GHOST HUNTING

MICHIGAN

Ghost Hunting Michigan

First edition 2012
Second edition 2025

Cover and interior design: Hilary Harkness
Editor: Annie Long and Andrew Mollenkof
Proofreader: Jenna Barron and Holly Cross
Typesetter: Karla Linder

Front cover and interior photos provided by the author unless otherwise noted.
All photos/illustrations copyright of their respective photographers.
Green background by **RODINA OLENA/shutterstock.com**
Chapter line design by **NATALIA-P/shutterstock.com**
Page viii: **Kenneth Keifer/shutterstock.com**
ADK branding background by **chyworks/shutterstock.com**

Front cover: **Extezy/shutterstock.com:** design line; **ZillaDigital/shutterstock.com:** diamond pattern; **NATALIA-P/shutterstock:** corner flourishes; **Tirta Sudibya /shutterstock.com:** AHRT antique car; **Zvezdesign/shutterstock.com:** "Ghost Hunting" vector font
Back cover: **Lario Tus/shutterstock.com:** background photo

Cataloging-in-Publication Data on file with the Library of Congress
ISBN 978-1-57860-430-2 (pbk.); 978-1-57860-431-9 (ebook)

CLERISY PRESS
an imprint of AdventureKeen
2204 First Ave. S., Ste. 102
Birmingham, AL 35233
800-678-7006; fax 877-374-9016

Visit **clerisypress.com** for a complete listing of our books and for ordering information.

Distributed by Publishers Group West
Printed in China

SAFETY NOTICE: Although Clerisy Press and the author have made every attempt to ensure that the information in this book is accurate at press time, they are not responsible for any loss, damage, injury, or inconvenience that may occur to anyone while using this book. Note that conditions can change from day to day. Minimize your risk on any ghost-hunting expedition by being knowledgeable, prepared, and alert.

HELEN PATTSKYN

GHOST HUNTING MICHIGAN

YOUR TRAVEL GUIDE TO THE STATE'S MOST HAUNTED PLACES

CLERISY PRESS

TABLE *of* CONTENTS

100-year-old Seul Choix Pointe Lighthouse is reportedly one fo the scariest haunted places in Michigan.

WELCOME TO AMERICA'S HAUNTED ROAD TRIP

DO YOU BELIEVE IN GHOSTS?

If you are like many Americans, you believe that ghosts walk among us. A CivicScience survey reports that 41% of US adults said they believe in ghosts or spirits, and a solid majority (64%) said they believe in at least one kind of paranormal or supernatural phenomenon. Perhaps you have heard your name called in a dark and empty house. It could be that you have awoken to the sound of footsteps outside your bedroom door, only to find no one there. It is possible that you saw your grandmother sitting in her favorite rocking chair, the same grandmother who had passed away several years before. Maybe you took a photo of a crumbling, deserted farmhouse and discovered strange mists and orbs in the photo, anomalies that were not visible to your naked eye.

If you have experienced similar paranormal events, then you know that ghosts exist. Even if you have not yet experienced these things, you are curious about the paranormal world, the spirit realm. If you weren't, you would not now be reading this preface.

Over the years, I have investigated haunted locations across the country, and with each new site, I found myself becoming more fascinated with ghosts. What are they? How do they manifest themselves? Why are they here? These are just a few of the questions I have been asking. No doubt, you have been asking the same questions.

The books in the America's Haunted Road Trip series from Clerisy Press can help you find the answers to your questions about ghosts. We've gathered some of America's top ghost writers (no pun intended) and researchers and asked them to write about their states' favorite haunts. Each location that they write about is open to the public so that you can visit them for yourself and try out your ghost-hunting skills. In addition to telling you about their often hair-raising adventures, the writers have included maps and travel directions so that you can take your own haunted road trip.

People may think that Michigan is all about lakes and woods, hunting and fishing, cherry orchards and Motor City, but Helen Pattskyn's *Ghost Hunting Michigan* proves that the Great Lakes State is fertile ground for entities even more fantastic than the 1960 Edsel Ranger. This book is a spine-tingling trip through Michigan's small towns and lively cities, its historic sites and fun spots, all of them haunted. Ride shotgun with Helen as she seeks out ghosts of seamen—the crew of the *Edmund Fitzgerald*—at the Whitefish Point Lighthouse and Shipwreck Museum and the spirits of thespians who took their final bows long ago at the Baldwin Theatre in Royal Oak. Travel with her to Camp Ticonderoga where a top-hatted phantom sits at a table, waiting for service. If you're lucky—or, perhaps, unlucky—you might run into the ghost of jilted Minnie Quay at Forester Pier, on Lake Huron's shore. And who was that ghostly woman who walked right through a door at Bone Heads BBQ in Willis? Hang on tight—*Ghost Hunting Michigan* is a scary ride.

But once you've finished reading this book, don't unbuckle your seat belt. There are still 49 states left for your haunted road trip! See you on the road!

John Kachuba
Editor, America's Haunted Road Trip

10
69
27
69
Fenton
Holly
75
94
23
Troy
Lansing
96
Royal Oak
127
Lake
St Clair
Detroit
Willis
Brownstown
12
75
127
223
23
LAKE ERIE
20
80
Ohio

SOUTHEASTERN MICHIGAN

CHAPTER 1

DETROIT

THE WHITNEY

When people think about Detroit, they often think of sports: the Tigers, the Red Wings, the Lions, and the Pistons. Or they think about the auto industry because Detroit is still "Motor City." It's also the home of Motown Records, where so many rock and roll greats got their start. Other people think of Detroit and remember the riots in the 1960s, or think about the crime rate, the problems with the school system, and all the rundown neighborhoods. When I think of Detroit, I think of shopping at Eastern Market for fresh produce— My husband is convinced that we have to arrive by 5 a.m., or "all the good stuff will be gone." I always tell him I'll take my chances, we don't *really* need to get there before 8 a.m. The Eastern Market's biggest day is on Saturday, and Saturdays are for sleeping in. My other favorite places in the city are the Detroit Public Library, the Detroit Institute of Art, the Opera House, the Symphony Hall, the Fox Theatre, and, of course, the Whitney restaurant.

Located on Woodward Avenue, just a few blocks from the campus of Wayne State University and Detroit's cultural center, the Whitney was once one of the city's oldest and most beautiful private residences. Now it is one of the city's finest and most beautiful restaurants. I've only been there to eat on a couple of very special occasions, but I fell immediately in love with the grand old house. Of course, prior to my visit on a bright sunny afternoon one April, I had only gone in looking for after-theater drinks and dessert with friends, not hoping for a glimpse of the ghost of former owner, David Whitney Jr.

Construction on the 52-room, Romanesque-style home began in 1890 and was completed four years later. One local newspaper described the house as "the most elaborate and substantial residence in this part of the country." The exterior walls of the mansion are made of South Dakota jasper, a rare type of pink granite. Inside, the first thing visitors see is the immense staircase in the Grand Hall, with its beautiful Tiffany stained glass panels, and a huge, ornate fireplace. There are 19 other fireplaces throughout the house, a secret vault hidden in the original dining room, and an elevator. A *haunted* elevator, according to stories. But ghosts aside, the Whitney mansion was one of the first homes of its day to boast such a modern convenience.

David Whitney Jr. was born in 1830 and came to Detroit at the age of 27, in 1857; he died in 1900, but his family continued to live in the house until the 1920s, when it was sold and became the home of the Wayne County Medical Society, which in turn later sold it to the Visiting Nurses Association some years later. In 1980, Richard Kughn purchased the property, and after six years of restoration, the Whitney opened up as "an American restaurant in an American palace." Kughn sold the property in 2007 to Bud Liebler, who continues to carry on the tradition of excellence started by his predecessor. In addition to the beautiful dining rooms on the main floor, there are outdoor garden parties all summer long, and the Ghost Bar up on the third floor.

When I spoke to David, one of the many wonderful staff members, I asked him if he had ever had any unusual experiences while working there—or if maybe any of his coworkers had seen or heard anything out of the ordinary.

"We have a lot of the usual stuff, I guess," he told me. "Doors sometimes shut as if by themselves. And one woman who used to work here told me that she was walking through the Great Hall, and one of the crystals, from one of the chandeliers, fell right at her feet and shattered. It kind of freaked her out a bit. Of course that might not have had anything to do with anything supernatural," he cautioned. "And if you knew her . . . she's a bit of a spirit herself," he added with a chuckle.

Ah, yes, I've known people like that, too.

David went on to tell me that a ghost-hunting team had been in a couple of times and spent the night, investigating the building. "They said that they heard a piano playing late at night, after all the staff had gone home. I think that would have been Grace Whitney. Grace was David Whitney's favorite daughter and quite an accomplished musician," he explained. "She played several instruments, and, in fact, the Whitneys used to open up the house and hold recitals so people could come and listen to her playing. Anyway, Grace was overseas when her father took ill. Of course, back then, you couldn't just hop on a plane and come home, so by the time she got here, he'd already died. The Ghost Hunters said they also picked up a male voice that same night, saying *I'm still here.* That was probably David Whitney."

The "infamous" second-floor elevator door at the Whitney

Of course, one of the most haunted places in the building is said to be the elevator, especially where it opens up onto the second floor. Not only did David Whitney Jr. pass away in the house, his wife, Sara, also died there. Numerous employees have reported that the elevator will start moving on its own and that the doors open and close without anyone pushing the button.

I asked if it would be all right to have a look around and take some photographs—although there are several public areas up on both the second and third floors, I like to ask permission, especially before taking pictures. I was welcomed to take as many photos as I liked and to go anywhere that wasn't marked "private." Of course, I would behave myself, I always do—but what I wouldn't have given for a tour of the *whole* house.

I wandered up to the second floor and took a couple of photos of the elevator before exploring every open-to-the-public room, just because I love old architecture and antiques. Finally, I meandered up the stairs to the third floor and the aptly named Ghost Bar. The bar wasn't open yet, but the bartender was setting up. He gave me a friendly "hello" and asked how I was doing.

"I'm doing great, thanks," I answered. Then I told him that I was writing a book about haunted places and that, naturally, the Whitney had come up.

The bartender smiled. "As long as you remember that everything I tell you is hearsay—that nothing's official—I've got a couple of stories for you, if you have a second and are interested."

"Absolutely." I was very interested and I had somehow managed to find unmetered parking on a nearby side street, so I had all afternoon!

"I've been a bartender here for about a year," he began, "and customers are always asking me if I've ever seen anything weird—you know, anything 'ghostly.' I haven't. But I've had some customers who said they did."

He told me that the first incident had occurred during a wedding in which the entire mansion had been rented out. "The way they run it is pre-dinner drinks are up here, then they serve dinner downstairs, and then we reopen the bar for post-dinner drinks," he told me. "There weren't very many children at this wedding, but there was this one little girl. She was maybe five or six and she kept running around and she didn't want to sit still. Her mom asked me if I'd mind keeping an eye on her for a few minutes, so she could go down and get something to eat. Everyone else had gone downstairs by then, and I really didn't mind, so I said 'sure,' and let the mom go downstairs. I left the little girl alone in this room, and I went into that room over there," he pointed to one of the sitting rooms adjacent to the bar.

"I was in there cleaning up, and all of the sudden, I heard this shriek, so I came running out to see what had happened. The little girl had this look on her face like she was totally terrified. I didn't see anyone—or anything—so I asked her what was wrong. She told me that a big ball of light had flown out of one corner of the room and came right at her. And she was really frightened," he emphasized. "This was before the 'Ghost Bar' sign was up, and she was way too young to know the history of the place—and way too young to make up something like that. She was okay after that, but I've never seen a little kid so scared."

The foyer of the Whitney

The bartender went on to tell me about another incident that happened about a month after that wedding reception, this time with a little boy who came upstairs with his mother. "He was right about the same age, too, I think. I didn't pay too much attention to them; they were just looking around. Then all of a sudden, I see this little boy dart out of that room and into the other room. I probably still wouldn't have thought too much of it, except I overheard him telling his mother, 'Mommy, Mommy, there it goes!' A few seconds later the mother came over to me and said that she was so sorry, but her son kept insisting he was being chased around by a ball of light."

The third incident involved an adult, a guy who had been sitting at the bar having a drink. "He was about my age," said the bartender, which would probably have made his customer somewhere in his mid-20s. "And he was talking on his cell phone, making plans to meet up with his buddies somewhere downtown. I turned away to take care of another customer. The next thing I knew this guy had jumped up out of his seat and was standing way over there, looking really freaked out. I asked him if he was okay, and he insisted that, yeah, he was fine. 'Are you sure?' I asked a second time. He looked pretty shaken up and I thought—I don't know, maybe he'd seen a mouse or something. This is an old building. 'No, I'm good, bro,' he told me. But he didn't sit back down. Instead, he told me he was ready to cash out."

The bartender said that as his customer was settling up his tab, he'd finally calmed down enough to admit that he'd seen the silhouette of a man standing behind him in the mirror behind the bar—but when he turned around, nobody was there.

Before I left, he took me over to one of the two side rooms—the one opposite the bar—and told me that that room was the one where people have complained about feeling "negative energy."

"Especially women," he told me. "When they come up here, they're just not comfortable in this room."

We talked for a few more minutes about paranormal phenomena in general, and I took a few more photographs before leaving the mansion.

Just a few blocks down from the Whitney is the Majestic Theatre, which is more than just a theater, I discovered when I popped in for a quick visit. I found both a café and a bowling alley—sadly, I didn't find any credible ghost stories. Still, the stage of the Majestic Theatre is the last place where Harry Houdini played before he died, and it's well worth checking out if you're in the area.

SPORTS BAR
MARLOW'S
CHILL & GRILL

CHAPTER 2

BROWNSTOWN

MARLOW'S CHILL & GRILL

When you mention the downriver area, most Detroiters think of the Gibraltar Trade Center, Flat Rock Speedway, Trenton Scarecrow Festival, or Cruisin' Downriver, an antique car event that rivals the northern suburb's Woodward Dream Cruise. Crusin' Downriver, which draws in thousands of spectators each summer, stretches to Lincoln Park, Wyandotte, Southgate, and Riverview.

Most people don't think about ghosts when you mention the downriver area, especially if you happen to be talking about the township of Brownstown. But that's exactly where I ended up one Monday afternoon in late November, on the trail of a promising lead I found through Motor City Ghost Hunters. I took my husband along for the ride, telling him it would make for a fun date. We hadn't been out to eat in a while, and even though a sports bar wouldn't normally be our first choice for a date night, we both love a good burger. He was a little dubious at first, not because he knew I was going on another one of my "ghost-hunting adventures," but because, unlike me, he is simply not a very adventurous soul. The idea of a 45-minute trek downriver for a burger wasn't exactly the highlight of his day. He decided to come anyway.

Marlow's is located on a rural stretch of Telegraph Road, just a short way down from the Oak Ridge Cemetery, which rumor has it is also haunted. According to an urban legend, the ghosts of a little boy and a tall man can be spotted in the cemetery between the hours of 9 p.m. and 3 a.m.—however, it is worth noting that like most cemeteries, Oak Ridge is closed after dark, and trespassers will be prosecuted. Visiting the cemetery during the day is perfectly legal, of course.

Other specters are said to roam the streets of the nearly 200-year-old town. Rumors abound of "strange apparitions" that supposedly wander the streets of the Tele Valley mobile home park and of a "ghostly man" who has allegedly been seen roaming the woods in Dawnshire Park near the Civic Center. Again, I don't recommend visiting either location after dark, but it's perfectly legal to walk around the Civic Center during the day. Just remember, you can't believe everything you read on the Internet, especially when it comes to ghostly hauntings. I learned that when I visited Calumet and Eagle Harbor earlier in the year.

It was early evening when we arrived in Brownstown and found ourselves in front of a large, beige brick-and-wood paneled building bearing a sign that read Marlow's Chill & Grill. I have to admit, I wasn't expecting the drive to be worth it; Marlow's does not *look* like a 100-year-old haunted tavern, even if it does have a rather colorful history. The building has served many functions, under many different owners, over the last century. In addition to being the home of numerous pubs and taverns, the building at one time housed a brothel in the upstairs apartment, and at another point in history, it served as a station house for the Brownstown mounted police. When we got there, the parking lot was mostly empty. For a moment I wondered if the place was open. As usual, I hadn't called ahead.

We parked anyway and headed up to the door to discover that yes, they were open, just not very busy yet. (At this point, my husband really wanted to know what I'd dragged him into!) Inside, Marlow's was everything you would expect from a friendly blue-collar neighborhood sports bar. Several televisions hung over the bar, sports memorabilia dotted the walls, and there was even a dance floor. In addition to bar seating, we found booths along one wall and had a seat. We didn't have long to wait before a friendly server came over to greet us with a smile and a couple of menus. Our server's name was Ashley. As we were talking, I learned that she had worked at Marlow's for a while. But before asking about the bar's resident specters, I decided what I really wanted was dinner. Ashley took our orders and put them into the kitchen. When she returned to check on us, I told her the real reason for my visit.

"This place is totally freaky!" she exclaimed. It took no prompting at all to get Ashley to tell me about some of the things she and other staff members had experienced at the bar. "We think one of the ghosts is a waitress who was murdered at the bar. The story I heard was that it was a customer who killed her. She was sitting on one of the bar stools, and he came up behind her and slit her throat."

No one has ever been able to dig up enough hard evidence to prove that someone was really murdered on the property, but it seems to be a widely held belief. Ashley told me that sometimes glasses fall off the shelves for no apparent reason, usually by the ice maker. "One night, I was standing right there," she went on, pointing over to the bar. "I think I'd been here for a couple of months, so I guess it was maybe last August. Anyway, I swear, I felt someone touching my face, like this," she demonstrated, sliding one finger down the side of her face, from her hairline all the way to her chin. "It freaked me right out."

Marlow's other resident specter is a much more negative entity, according to paranormal investigators and bar staff alike. He can be felt most strongly around the ladies restroom and in the upstairs apartment, which is no longer used for anything except storage. Ashley said that most of the staff avoids the apartment and hardly anyone will go up there alone. "*No one* would live there," she added.

"One night, after closing," she continued, "the night bartender literally came *running* out of the bathroom, screaming. She said she'd been in the stall and felt somebody running their fingers through her hair like they were standing behind her."

Okay, that would be enough to shake me up, too, and I don't rattle that easily. Ashley told me that a number of staff members and even some customers have felt as if they were being watched in and around the restrooms (even when there was no one else around), and a few have also reported being touched, although the night bartender's experience was by far the most extreme. Most of what the staff experiences seems to happen when they're cleaning up, after closing.

But what I wanted to know more about was the apartment upstairs. Being the brave soul that I am, I asked if it would be all right to go up and take pictures. Ashley said she didn't think it would be a problem, but she put in a call to the owner, Robert Marlow, just to double-check.

About then, our food was ready, so while Ashley called her boss, I scribbled down a few notes and my husband dug into his burger. "Well?" I asked him.

He wasn't sure if I was asking about the burger or the ghosts, so he just shrugged. As far as *I* was concerned, the ghost stories were more than worth the drive downriver. (But I enjoyed my dinner too.)

When Ashley returned, she let me know that Marlow didn't mind me going upstairs. The only catch was that nobody had a key, so would I mind coming back tomorrow? Not at all!

While I munched on my fries, Ashley told us about the Motor City Ghost Hunters' visit in 2010. "They were here most of the night with all their equipment. They're the ones who told us that there were two different spirits, the woman at the bar and the other one upstairs. They got a bunch of stuff on tape." They were able to capture a picture of an orb that they caught downstairs in the bar area and audio of the EVP (electronic voice phenomena) they encountered during their visit.

By then other customers were drifting in, so Ashley left us to finish our food. I did visit the ladies' room before we left, but, alas, if the ghost was about, he wasn't in the mood to play with any customers that night.

I returned the next afternoon and was shown around back by the bar's manager. He unlocked the door to the upstairs storage area, flipped on the light, and with hardly a word, retreated hastily back into the bar. Maybe he was too busy to accompany me upstairs, but I had to admit it was a little odd, being left to wander around on my own like that, even though Ashley was right about there not being much upstairs. The upper floor of Marlow's was clearly hardly used at all. I took a number of photographs and left my digital recorder switched on, hoping I might see or hear something interesting. No such luck. I didn't feel especially uneasy, either. Maybe I'll have better luck somewhere else.

Before I left, I made sure to lock up. I thanked Ashley again for all her help and promised her that the next time I'm downriver, I'll stop back by for a burger . . . and maybe take another shot at ghost hunting!

CHAPTER 3

TROY

CAMP TICONDEROGA

I first discovered Camp Ticonderoga a decade or so ago. At the time, I was waiting tables at a little Coney Island restaurant in Royal Oak, and, like most waitresses, I kept tabs on my regular customers—their names, their usual order, where they worked, etc. That's how I met S. (I haven't seen him in years, so I couldn't ask him if it was all right to use his name.) It was pretty obvious what S. did for a living the first time he came in wearing a chef's coat and checked pants, so I asked him where he worked.

"Camp Ticonderoga," he told me.

"I have friends who eat there all the time. They told me it's haunted."

I hadn't actually taken my friends very seriously, but S. looked me dead in the eye and said, "Yeah, that's Hannah. Everybody at Camp Ti knows her."

I didn't believe S. any more than I believed my friends. "Come on, you *really* expect me to believe your workplace is haunted?" Surely, S. and his coworkers were mistaking the sounds of an old building settling for the sounds of ghosts. But S. assured me that he didn't believe in ghosts either before he started working there.

It didn't take long before he changed his mind, however. "Lights flicker on and off all the time, and I swear the elevator has a mind of its own," he told me. "The elevator door opens and shuts when no one is even near it, let alone in it. Sometimes other doors slam shut, and dishes fall off the shelves in the kitchen," he added.

Needless to say, I was intrigued, so I decided to check it out—besides, the food was supposed to be pretty good, so at worst, I'd be disappointed in the ghost but get a good meal.

On my next day off, I drove up Rochester Road and arrived at the sprawling old farmhouse-turned-restaurant a little before the dinner rush. As soon as I was settled at a table, I asked my waitress if the place was really haunted. "Oh, yes, absolutely." She told me the same things my friend the chef had, adding that Hannah had lived in the house around the turn of the century. The story was that she hanged herself from the rafters in one of the bedrooms—that area is now a part of the upstairs dining room. I was glad I was on the main floor.

"Why did she kill herself?" I asked.

"I don't think anyone knows."

I didn't think much about Camp Ti or Hannah again until I started writing about Michigan's haunted places and decided that it was past time to revisit the restaurant.

The building was originally a farmhouse that belonged to Elizabeth and Henry Blount and was built in the early 1820s, just after the city of Troy was settled. Elizabeth and Henry raised seven children in the large two-story home and eventually passed the property down to their grandsons, Harry and Frank. The Blount family continued to live in the home until May 13, 1924, when the farm was sold and ultimately developed into the Sylvan Glen Golf Course. The developers turned the old farmhouse into a restaurant. It has had many different names over the decades, including the Double Eagle, the Wooden Horse, and the Shark Creek Inn. In 1996, it became Camp Ticonderoga—or Camp Ti, for short.

According to their website, the restaurant is "an upscale, yet rustic, bar and grill . . . Camp Ti boasts a comfortable, inviting Adirondack atmosphere. . . ." That description doesn't really do justice to the rugged log-cabin interior with its three huge stone fireplaces, antler chandeliers, and mounted hunting trophies on the walls. My favorite part of the décor is right inside the door, where you'll find Camp Ti's "dog wall." The owners are self-avowed "dog people" and love to have their customers bring in pictures of their canine companions. Once a month a "mutt of the month" is chosen and the lucky dog gets a doggy bag filled with goodies from the kitchen.

For its human clientele, Camp Ti serves up a variety of menu options, ranging from salads and homemade soups to Black Angus steak and specials such as traditional shepherd's pie, "buffaloaf" (buffalo meatloaf), and venison stew. Throughout the year, Camp Ti hosts a number of themed parties, including its annual "beach bash" in March. Guests are encouraged to wear their favorite Hawaiian shirt and play on an artificial beach. Anyone who lives in Michigan knows that by March, we're ready for a little "sun and sand," even if we have to create it ourselves.

I could have used some sun and sand myself, on the cold, snowy winter day I chose to return to Camp Ticonderoga, on my hunt for more stories about Hannah. I went in for lunch and got a quiet table overlooking the golf course. And it was just my luck—I got the *one* waitress who was even more skeptical than I am about the paranormal. I told her about the book I was writing and asked her about Hannah. Her response was an almost apologetic confession: "I don't believe in ghosts."

I asked her if she would mind explaining why she felt that way. "I'm not out to prove or disprove anything," I promised. "I'm just gathering peoples' stories. It might make a good balance to hear from someone who doesn't believe this place is haunted."

"It's an old building," my waitress reminded me. "So if the lights flicker I figure it's just the wiring. The elevators are old too, so if the doors open and shut unexpectedly, it's just a mechanical thing. I've never felt creeped out anywhere in the restaurant. People are always making something out of nothing, you know?"

Fair enough, but I still hoped to talk to someone about Hannah—after all, I had already met several people who were convinced she still haunted Camp Ti. My server was happy to help out by introducing me to the manager on duty. The restaurant was starting to get a little busy by then, so I exchanged business cards with the manager and arranged to come back another time. In the end, I was put in touch with assistant manager, Christy Hardy, who, I was told, had been at Camp Ti for about 10 years and was something of an expert when it came to Hannah. She had also had a few personal experiences with Hannah—and apparently some other ghosts as well.

Christy met me the following Sunday afternoon—she was very sweet and quite happy to give me a few minutes of her time. After getting us each a glass of soda, she settled us at a quiet table near the second bar, toward the back of the restaurant so we could talk. I explained my book and asked her what she could tell me about Camp Ticonderoga's ghosts.

"When I first started here, I remember walking up the stairs to the second floor and seeing a man sitting at a table, near the staircase. I thought it was a little odd, as no one was supposed to be up there; that part of the dining room was closed. He was dressed kind of funny too, in a vintage suit, like something you'd have seen a hundred years ago, and he was wearing a top hat. And then suddenly, he was gone." She explained that she was a little freaked out, but then another manager said she had seen the same man sitting there on a different occasion. "We had another manager quit, after just a couple of days," she added. "I don't know why, but . . ." she shrugged, leaving it open-ended.

The man in the top hat wasn't the only ghost the staff has reported seeing—or experiencing in other ways.

Christy told me about a server who had napkin-wrapped silverware roll right off the table upstairs. "She didn't think too much of it at first, she just picked it up and put a clean roll in its place. That rolled off the table too. It happened twice more, really freaking her out. There are several people who won't go upstairs by themselves."

Christy went on, "Some people claim to have been touched, but when they turn to see who's there, there isn't anyone nearby. And a lot of people have experienced cold spots upstairs. It's like you'll be walking along and suddenly get freezing cold for no reason." She also said that several people, both guests and staff, have reported hearing footsteps on the staircase leading up to the second floor. "But when they turn around, there's no one there. People hear children's voices too. And we have a ghost cat," she added, telling me how numerous people have reported hearing it meowing, especially when there aren't many customers around and the restaurant is quiet.

"One day I heard it and I was so sure it was a real cat that had gotten stuck up in the attic, I asked one of the cooks to go check it out. When he came down, he said that there was no cat. There wasn't any evidence that any kind of animal had gotten in recently, either."

I had to admit, it seemed like there was an awful lot of seemingly supernatural activity at Camp Ticonderoga. It was little wonder the place had been investigated by so many paranormal investigators.

Christy explained to me that she's not really afraid of the ghosts, but sometimes locking up alone at night is a little nerve-wracking. She said she preferred to turn the lights off in the back first and then make her way toward the front door so that the last lights to go off are the ones nearest the doors. She also repeated the story I'd heard before about how sometimes doors around the restaurant seem to open and shut by themselves. "One night it happened to me after closing, and I kept calling 'Who's there?' but no one answered. No one was here."

There was another night, Christy told me, when she locked up and headed toward her car in the parking lot. She chanced to turn around and glance back at the building and swore that she saw a pair of blue glowing eyes watching her in the window. "Those windows there, behind the bar," she told me, pointing to the windows behind the main bar area. She didn't go back in to investigate. I wasn't sure I blamed her; I doubt I would have gone back in, either.

CHAPTER 4

ROYAL OAK

BALDWIN THEATRE

When I was living practically within walking distance of the Baldwin Theatre, I decided to take a chance and dropped in unannounced, even though it was close to Christmas. I knew there was a good chance I might not get to actually talk to anyone that day—but it was a good excuse to walk around downtown Royal Oak and get some last-minute shopping done.

I arrived at the Baldwin during regular box office hours and was greeted by Vonnie Miller. As soon as I explained the reason for my visit, she invited me into the office to talk. Unfortunately, she was the only person in just then and couldn't actually show me around, but Vonnie confirmed that the theater was "very haunted." She added that the Baldwin has been in a couple of books and has hosted several "haunted" events, where the audience is presented with the theater's history, along with its ghost stories.

I'd already read several newspaper articles about the Baldwin's ghosts and knew that the theater was a favorite stop on Halloween "ghost tours," as well as a favorite stop for paranormal investigators. There have been numerous pictures of orbs taken on both stages, as well as EVP (electronic voice phenomena) recordings of strange voices, and reports of sharp drops in temperature throughout the theater. It seems that when ghosts are around, the ambient temperature drops significantly. These so-called "cold spots" are a good indication of paranormal activity—after

you've ruled out all of the logical explanations, like open doors or drafty windows.

Vonnie told me whom I really needed to talk to was Development Director Lesley Branden-Phillips. Lesley was off for the Christmas holiday, but Vonnie gave me her card and suggested I call the following week to set up an appointment.

I took advantage of the bright, mild afternoon to get some shots of the exterior of the building before heading off to do some Christmas shopping. Royal Oak is a hub for the arts community in Oakland County and has been one of my favorite places to visit since I was a teenager. Summer is my favorite time to be there, when the streets are crowded with pedestrians, making it a great time to people-watch. No matter what time of year it is, though, there's always something fun and interesting happening in Royal Oak.

In March, classical music lovers can enjoy the Baroque Music Festival, while cinema buffs can travel a couple of miles up Woodward Avenue to enjoy the Uptown Film Festival. April brings Royal Oak's annual Earth Day/Green Living festival to the Detroit Zoo (which is actually located in the city of Royal Oak). June is marked by an annual fine-art fair, but the big arts event is in late August, when more than 200 musical acts fill up ten stages on Royal Oak's streets for the Arts, Beats, and Eats festival. For more great food, visit in November for the Annual Royal Oak Chili Cook-Off, where professional chefs and amateurs alike compete for the title of the best chili in town. One of these years, I'm going to convince my husband to enter.

Even when there isn't a fair or festival going on, Royal Oak's shopping district—about a mile-long stretch down the city's two main roads, Washington and Main Street—is filled with dozens of specialty boutiques, art galleries, vintage-clothing stores, and an amazing variety of restaurants, pubs, and coffee shops. And in the heart of it all is the Baldwin Theatre, home of the Stagecrafters community theater company. The Stagecrafters originally called the nearby city of Clawson their home. They began there in 1956, when Clawson residents Robert Johnson, then a sophomore at Michigan State University, and Sally Bosz, a senior at Clawson High School, decided to start a summer theater program. With a cast and crew of only 30 people, the company—then known as the Clawson Community Club Players—performed Noel Coward's *Blithe Spirit* as a part of Clawson's annual Fourth of July celebration. The play was performed in the Clawson Elementary gymnasium and was declared "a hit" by local newspapers.

Because of the success of its first production, the company decided it needed to move to a bigger venue and was granted the use of the auditorium at Madison Heights' John Page Middle School. With the move to a new city, the troupe decided to change its name, and in 1957 the Stagecrafters company was officially born.

Over the next decade, the troupe grew and eventually returned to Clawson, where they purchased an old church on Bowers Street. The first play to debut at the Bowers Street Playhouse was Joseph Kesselring's *Arsenic and Old Lace;* the year was 1971. The company continued to grow, and in 1983 the Stagecrafters were invited by the International Amateur Theatre Association to take part in an exchange program with a theater troupe in England. They visited St. Albans the following year to perform on the stage of the Abbey Theatre.

By the following year, they knew it was time to move again; they needed a bigger theater with more space for rehearsals, a larger stage, and more room for building sets. When the city of Royal Oak offered them the Baldwin Theatre, the company took up a collection for the down payment, took out a mortgage to cover the rest, and purchased the property. They renamed their theater "The Baldwin." The article on the Baldwin's home page describes the restoration of the old, long-abandoned building as both a "Herculean task" and a "labor of love"—after talking to Lesley it was easy to see that that wasn't an exaggeration.

After Christmas, I used the card I'd been given and set up an appointment to come back to the theater. Lesley, Vonnie's coworker, met me at the box-office door and walked me through the back halls to the lobby, and then onto the main stage. She told me that the Baldwin was originally a silent-movie house and that it was older than the more well-known Fox Theatre, in downtown Detroit. Also, when it was first built, back in 1922, "the Baldwin was considered the grandest theater in the Midwest." Looking out at the auditorium from the main stage, I had no difficulty believing that.

"All of this has been restored," Lesley said, as I was admiring the architectural décor, much of it reminiscent of Greek murals. "All of the murals you're looking at were covered up by truly awful-looking yellow curtains—we had *no* idea what we would find behind them. It was a pleasant surprise, but it was a lot of work to make this place beautiful again." The walls, Lesley told me, had been painted in what could only be described as a hideous shade of "blood red."

The Main Stage auditorium of the Baldwin Theatre

"The auditorium originally seated 1,400 guests, but we knew a community theater would never need that much seating, so we created the lobby area at the back and turned the mezzanine into our lighting and tech booth."

Lesley also told me that the Baldwin's pipe organ—once a staple in silent-movie houses—was still operational and that they host a couple of pipe organ concerts each year. "We have one of the few functioning pipe organs in the state," she added. As she continued with the theater's history, I learned that after the silent-movie era, the Baldwin hosted vaudeville performances. "Rumor has it Houdini performed here," said Lesley, "but it's *just* a rumor." In the 1950s, the Baldwin was converted over to "talkies"—talking pictures—and first-run movies were shown. But by the 1960s, the theater began its long, slow decline, showing only second-run films. The theater finally shut down after a fire in 1984. It was shortly thereafter that the city of Royal Oak sold the theater to the Stagecrafters, and they began their long and loving restoration process.

In addition to the main stage on the first floor, there is a second, smaller stage built into the old balcony area, behind the lighting/tech booth, where smaller productions are shown.

Lesley told me that she's had a number of paranormal investigators come through and has heard lots of stories from employees and patrons alike about ghosts. She invited me to follow her backstage and explained that quite a few people have claimed to hear "deliberate, slow" footsteps in the wings, just under the rigging, even though no one else was anywhere nearby. Next, she led the way downstairs to the "green room," where actors hang out between scenes. It's also where the Stagecrafters's costumers work, creating wardrobes for each of the company's productions—as many as ten plays per year on both stages and as a part of their youth program.

"What most people don't know is that this used to be a fallout shelter," Lesley added, as we walked down the narrow stairs. It's also where there has been the most spectral activity in the past. "People have said they felt like they were being watched. I've even had people say they felt like someone had touched them down here," said Lesley.

She pointed out the door to the orchestra pit and said that when she first came to the theater, no one seemed to be able to photograph it clearly. Pictures were always distorted or clouded over; many had orbs in them. "It's been quiet the last couple of years," she added, explaining that in the beginning, she had so many people coming through that she wondered if maybe the ghosts got annoyed and went away—or at least decided to lie low for a while. "You're the first person I've had through here in almost a year." I felt both flattered and grateful to Lesley for giving me not only so much of her time but also allowing me to tour the theater and write about it.

She went on to tell me about one particular incident in which a theater worker came downstairs to find that all of the furniture and a bunch of boxes that he'd stacked up earlier in the day had all been moved to the center of the room. At first, he assumed the actors or staff members were pulling a prank, but everyone who was there denied having anything to do with it. Not only was the man in question one of the most honest people Lesley said she'd ever worked with, but also he didn't see any reason to doubt his colleagues—and there hadn't been very many people around that day, anyway.

Lesley led the way through a labyrinth of corridors to the wig and makeup rooms, back up the stairs to the lobby, and up to the second stage. "We've probably had as much activity up here as down in the green room," she told me, although the second stage has also been quiet the last few years.

Lesley told me about one man's particularly harrowing experience in the second stage area. Behind the stage is the lighting/tech booth, for the lower, main stage. One of the stagehands was going about his business when he got locked in the booth—the door *should* have opened, but he said it seemed "stuck." For the next several minutes, he heard loud pounding, like someone beating their palms or fists up against the walls from the outside—when he finally got the door open, no one was anywhere to be seen.

She told me that on another occasion, the technicians came in to find the lights above the second stage had been moved around overnight, and instead of pointing at the stage, they were pointing at the ceiling. Not only was the building locked up and empty overnight, but the theater lights were big, heavy pieces of equipment. They're also pretty high up off the floor. It takes special equipment and usually a couple of people working together to move them; it certainly couldn't have been the job of a lone prankster.

Finally, Lesley pointed out a door off to the left, behind the seating area, telling me that there have been a number of sightings of an apparition in the doorway. I decided that it would make a good picture for the book—but the brand-new batteries that I had just put in my camera that morning were dead . . . proof? Who knows, but I *had* been saying ever since staying overnight at the Blue Pelican (see Chapter 21) that I would love to experience something a little more "concrete" for myself. Maybe the ghosts of the Baldwin Theatre decided to come out of hiding to grant my wish.

CHAPTER 5

WILLIS

BONE HEADS BBQ

I was sitting around with some friends the week after Easter talking about the book I was writing. Everybody knew about the project, knew my deadline was fast approaching, and was excited to hear how it was going. They weren't saying "no" if I happened to offer up a couple of ghost stories, either. One of them even had a ghost story for me.

"We were at Bone Heads BBQ a few months ago," my friend Jayne told me. "And my son *swore* he saw a guy standing by the foot of the stairs leading up to the second floor. When I looked up, I didn't see anything, but when he told our waitress about it, she said it was probably one of the ghosts."

I've known Jayne long enough to consider her reliable, even if I've never met her teenage son. "So where is this place?" I asked.

She grinned. "Ypsilanti, I think. I can't remember which road—you can probably find it online."

When I got home, I did a quick Internet search and found out that Bone Heads BBQ is actually in Willis, a tiny community that's little more than a dot on the map, just south of Ypsilanti Charter Township. I mapped out my route, packed my gear and an overnight bag, and headed westward on I-94 once again. Willis is actually within easy driving distance of metro Detroit, but I like to be prepared and was planning a couple of other stops along the way.

I timed my arrival at Bone Heads for lunch because I love BBQ-style food, but I nearly missed my destination and had

to turn around. The restaurant did not look like much from the outside, and the town around it consisted of little more than railroad tracks, a post office, and a few streets of older-looking homes. But sometimes the best food is served up in the most out-of-the-way places.

The exterior of the old wood-sided building may have been unimpressive, but as soon as I walked in the door, I knew that I'd come to exactly the right place, both for lunch and ghost stories. The décor was reminiscent of an old general store, the atmosphere was relaxed, and the smells coming from the kitchen were enough to convince me I wouldn't be disappointed. I was greeted by a friendly server and told her that while I was definitely staying for lunch, that wasn't the real reason for my visit. I was writing a book about haunted places and wondered if there might be somebody there who could talk to me about ghosts.

She hesitated a moment before suggesting I should maybe check out their website.

Of course, I would definitely do that when I got back home. "But what I'm really hoping to get are some more personal stories," I went on. "Anything you've experienced, or maybe something one of your coworkers or customers has told you."

During my travels, I've learned that sometimes I've had to ask more than once. If someone says "no," or "not interested," I've backed off—some businesses really do not want a "haunted reputation." But sometimes people have hesitated either because they weren't sure what I was really asking them for, or because they didn't want to come off as sounding crazy. Sometimes just talking to folks for a few minutes was the best way to get them to open up.

This was one of those times. My waitress looked over at a woman who was walking through the dining room and asked her if she had a few minutes to talk to someone writing a book.

The second woman introduced herself as Niki LaChance, one of the owners. Niki said she had a few minutes, but she was really in the middle of getting ready for lunch, so she couldn't talk too long.

"That would be fantastic," I assured her. Before becoming a full-time writer, I was a full-time waitress, so I completely understood the restaurant business and that sometimes a few minutes is all someone has to spare.

Niki refilled her iced tea and showed me over to a table, telling me that she and her husband, Jim, had bought the business about three years ago. "We opened up on Friday the thirteenth," she said.

"That sounds auspicious," I joked.

She laughed too. "It was. Actually, I like to say we came here by fate," she added. The business had been struggling before they bought it, but Niki and Jim managed to turn Bone Heads into a thriving, friendly neighborhood restaurant. "We're definitely a 'destination location,'" she added when I mentioned almost missing the place. "There isn't much else around here."

Niki told me that the village of Willis was named after Willis Potter, one of the area's original landowners. "He came here around 1825."

She took me over to the staircase—the same staircase where my friend's son said he'd seen a ghost—leading up to the second floor to show me some of the old photos hanging on the wall.

"Originally, the building was a stagecoach stop," Niki said.

She told me that it was built in 1865 and had been the home of many different businesses over the course of the last century and a half. "It was a granary, a butcher shop, an ice house, a post office, a boarding house, and even a general store." Then she went on to tell me that the staircase is one of the most active areas in the restaurant. Maybe that was why I had the chills as we stood on the stairs talking—or was it because I'd already heard about a ghost hanging around the stairwell?

Numerous spirits have been spotted by guests on the steps leading upstairs at Bone Heads BBQ.

"One of the waitresses told me once that she was standing at the base of the stairs and felt someone touching her hair," said Niki. "She turned around expecting it to be one of the cooks messing with her—but no one was there.

"The building was completely restored back in the 1980s," Niki went on, emphasizing that it was restored, not renovated. The former owners wanted to recapture the feel of the original building. "They brought in antiques and fixtures from all over the state," she said, pointing out stained glass windows from an old church up north and a huge, old apothecary's cabinet on the far wall filled with antiques.

As she continued telling me about the restaurant's ghosts, it sounded as if more than just antiques were brought into the building when it was restored, however. Besides the man that my friend's son had seen around the staircase, Bone Heads is, according to the staff and customers, haunted by a pair of female specters. One of them is described as a teenage girl, who apparently came into the building along with that apothecary's cabinet. The other female ghost is an older woman they call Nellie, who has, according to Niki, been with the building for as long as anyone can remember. One of the cooks claimed to have seen Nellie walk across the kitchen and out the back door—literally going *through* the door.

"We have a ghost cat, too, named Pickles," said Nikki. "It was . . . 2009, I think. We'd just opened up, and I had a customer ask me why we allowed animals in the dining room. I told him that we *didn't*. He swore he saw a white cat walking along the back wall. Other customers have seen him over the years too."

Niki told me that they've had things like that happening from the very beginning. "One of the first things I personally witnessed was this big vase of flowers sliding right across one of the tables out on the sun porch. I was sitting right over there with three other people." She pointed to a table by the window. "The vase went from the middle of the table right over the edge and broke."

I had to admit, that seemed a little unusual.

"There was another time," Niki went on, "when a lady came out of the restroom really shaken up. I asked her what happened. She told me she'd been standing in front of the mirror—there's a wreath behind the mirrors. One of the glass globes on it just exploded. I made that wreath," she added. "I know how well the ornaments are glued in place. There's no reason for it to have just shattered like that. It didn't fall, it just . . . exploded."

That wasn't the only ghostly encounter someone had experienced in the ladies' restroom. Another time, Niki told me, one of the waitresses was in there by herself. "She told me that she dropped her cigarette lighter," said Nikki. The lighter must have slid across the floor because Niki said the waitress told her that as she was bending over to pick it up, it slid back to her, "like somebody had kicked it over to her."

I supposed incidents like that were why Niki categorized the restaurant's spirits as "friendly"—just a little mischievous from time to time. "Sometimes doors open and shut upstairs, or lights flicker. The old owners told me that sometimes the lights would sway back and forth in the bar for seemingly no reason at all," she added.

Then Niki told me that after they bought the place, she asked the former owner if she had ever had any unusual experiences in the restaurant. "She lived in the apartment upstairs," Niki explained. "She said that one morning she came down to get the paper from the front porch. She didn't realize it was raining until she got downstairs, so she went back up to get her slippers. When she came back down, she found the wet newspaper sitting on the inside of the locked front door."

Niki was also told that numerous people have seen "someone" cleaning the front upstairs windows—*after* the former owners moved out, but *before* Niki and her husband bought the place and moved into the upstairs apartment with their teenage daughter, Franchesca.

Antique humidor at Bone Heads BBQ

"What's it like living in a haunted building?" I asked.

"At first my daughter was a little nervous—and sometimes it's a little freaky when doors open up upstairs all by themselves. But the first thing I did when we moved in was ask God to watch over us and drive out anything bad. I figured the good spirits could stay, since they were here first. We haven't had any problems; they're just mischievous."

Niki pointed out the clock on the wall and said that it had come with the restaurant, but it had never worked. The previous owners weren't even sure it had "guts" or if it was just decorative.

"Then one night, at exactly eleven-thirty, it started bonging and the minute hand started to move. We were closed up for the night, all the lights were off, and there were just four of us in here. I'd just pulled the cash drawer and was taking it upstairs," she said. "I turned around because I couldn't figure out what the sound was at first. Then I realized it was the clock, and I called to the bartender and my brother-in-law, who were sitting in the bar area talking. I wanted them to see it. My brother-in-law got a chair and took the clock off the wall—all this time it had been bonging," she added. "But as soon as he touched it, it stopped, and suddenly the time read 5 o'clock. It hasn't made a sound or moved since then.

"And just recently," she went on, "It was about seven-thirty in the morning, and I'd gone out for a run. When I got back, Jim told me that he could have sworn he heard me come in, walk up the stairs, go into the office, and open up the liquor cabinet. The cabinet door squeaks," she explained. "It's a pretty distinctive sound. He wondered what I was doing, so he went into the office—only I wasn't back from my run yet. No one was in the office. The dog heard it too," she added. "Jim told me the dog started barking when he heard the footsteps on the stairs."

Niki said that they'd had a number of paranormal teams come out to investigate the place since they moved in. There have been a lot of orb photos taken as well as EVP (electronic voice phenomena) evidence and video clips, all of which can be accessed from Bone Heads website.

Just about then Patrice, Niki's office manager, came in. Niki called her over and explained what we were talking about, adding that Patrice had accompanied a couple of the paranormal teams when they were at the restaurant doing their investigations.

"Did you tell her about Bob?" Patrice asked.

"No, I almost forgot," said Niki. "Bob used to live in the attic, right at the top of the stairs—it's not much more than a crawl space, but I guess it used to be a bedroom. When the last team was out here they were communicating with him, weren't they?"

Patrice nodded. "I think I remember them saying Bob told them he used to work on the property as some kind of caretaker or maintenance man."

I wondered if maybe that was the apparition my friend's son had seen.

“Have you had any experiences?” Niki asked Patrice.

“Not really . . . well, there was that one time I was sitting here with a friend of mine. She’s really sensitive to stuff like this,” explained Patrice. “She said she saw a little girl tugging on the apron sting of one of the waitresses.”

Later on, when Patrice asked that particular waitress if she’d felt anything unusual that night, the young woman told her she’d felt a tugging on her apron string, but had just blown it off as “nothing.” Everyone agreed that was a little freaky. I thought so too.

SPOTLIGHT ON THE MOTOR CITY GHOST HUNTERS

When I visited the Whitefish Point Lighthouse and Shipwreck Museum, just as I was pulling in, the Motor City Ghost Hunters were pulling out. But before they could hit the road for the long trek back home, Beth, the housekeeper for the Crew Quarters at Whitefish Point, introduced us. I couldn't have met with a nicer or more knowledgeable group of people.

As I was wrapping up the last details of this book, I got back in touch with John, who is both the team's leader and founder, to thank him again for taking the time to talk with me that day back in September and to ask permission to use some of their information to put together a "Team Profile" for my book. He graciously gave me the go-ahead and filled me in on some of the things they've been up to since the last time we spoke.

Probably the most exciting news is that when the Ghost Hunters were going over their footage from Whitefish Point, they realized they'd caught what looked like an apparition on tape. Fox News ran the clip; it can also be seen on both the Ghost Hunters' website and on YouTube. John told me the footage had been turned over to SyFy's *Fact or Faked* for further investigation—but he was there that night and assured me that there was nothing "fake" about it. Not that I thought there might be. The Ghost Hunters may be believers in the paranormal, but they will always look for logical explanations first.

John said he and his teammates have been on investigations pretty much every weekend since September and have a lot more planned for the coming year, including visits to the Mansfield State Prison, Yankee Air Museum, and, of course, their annual visit to Whitefish Point. Also included in their busy schedule are a number of educational talks at local libraries, as well as a special event just for children who are interested in learning more about the paranormal.

John told me that he and his team always put children first, and any request for an investigation where kids are involved will always get top priority. "It's about letting people know they don't have to be afraid, especially in their own home or business," he said. The sentiment is echoed by every other member of the team. That desire to ease people's fears is what drives these folks to give up their weekends and free time. None of them are paid for what they do—yet they spend no small amount of money on equipment. Having talked to them at length, it was easy to see why they are so well respected.

John is a licensed mechanical contractor with certification in microbial pest management. In other words, he's pretty good at figuring out if what seems to be a ghostly phenomenon is "real" or if it can easily be explained away as something related to the structure of a building. Like many of his teammates, he has been interested in the paranormal for most of his life.

One of the other members I met at Whitefish Point was Chass. Like John, she's married with children and has experienced a number of things in her life that couldn't be easily or scientifically explained. Chass joined the team after the Motor City Ghost Hunters conducted an investigation in her home.

I also met lead investigator and case manager Kellie, who describes herself as both a "true believer" and a bit of a skeptic. Her educational background is in social science.

Of course, with more than two dozen team members, it would be impossible to mention them all. What I can say is that I look forward to seeing them again; I've been invited to join them on an investigation and have every intention of accepting that invitation as soon as time allows.

CHAPTER 6

HOLLY

HOLLY ANTIQUES

Holly Antiques is a lovely shop that now sits where Main Street Antiques once did. It's also one of the oldest buildings in Holly's historic district. In 2008, Lynn and Mark Hay purchased the business and were the owners until the business changed hands in 2016. The following entry recounts my visit to the store while it was still Main Street Antiques. Although the original antique shop has moved on, only time will tell whether the other residents have . . . or have not.

Main Street Antiques was home to 40 antique dealers selling an eccentric variety of heirlooms, antiques, artifacts, and collectibles, including some rather unusual merchandise. The first thing my husband spotted when we walked in the door was a vampire slaying kit. The kit, which Lynn speculated originated somewhere in Europe, contained rosaries, holy water, wooden stakes, a mallet, and even a revolver loaded with actual silver bullets. Leave it to my husband to find the strangest thing in the shop!

Lynn told me that sometimes she felt like her shop was "a magnet for the unusual." In addition to the vampire slaying kit, she had numerous Native American items and even real shrunken heads come into her store over the years. Looking around the store, it wasn't hard to find a few curiosities tucked in among the teacups, antique buttons, and costume jewelry. It was no wonder that prop masters from six movie production teams visited Lynn and Mark's shop to find just that "perfect piece" to complete a movie set.

The only things Lynn told me she would not allow in her shop were Ouija boards and tarot cards. She explained that she believed in the paranormal and that there were both good and bad spirits out there, but that certain items just naturally attract energy she didn't want around her. I had heard before how dangerous Ouija boards were because they somehow attracted malicious spirits. I had a friend many years ago who was absolutely petrified of "witch boards," as they are sometimes called.

Other people, of course, dismiss the boards as nothing more than hoaxes or parlor games. As for tarot cards, Lynn couldn't imagine why anyone would want to read with used tarot cards, anyway. "You never know the kind of person who owned them before you," she said.

After we chatted for a few minutes, Lynn invited us to follow her up to the second floor, where we could find a quieter place to talk. She led the way up the narrow wooden staircase, at the top of which sat a portrait of a little girl.

"A lot of people say they see a little girl running around up here," Lynn told me. "And we all hear footsteps coming from up here, like someone's walking around, even though there isn't anyone up here." She directed us to a corner by the windows overlooking Main Street, where she cleared the place settings off a 1970s-era wooden dinette table so we could sit and talk more comfortably.

I asked her a little bit about the shop.

"Mark has been in the antiques business for a long time," said Lynn. "So when we found out that this place was for rent and that the owners wanted it to remain an antiques shop, it just seemed like the right move to make.

"Antiques attract spirits; they get attached to them. Whenever something from a new dealer comes in, we notice a lot more activity. It's like the ghosts who have been here awhile feel like they need to 'check out' the new guys." Lynn also noted that spirits seem attracted to dolls and mirrors.

Another reason the shop might be so haunted, she speculated, is that the downstairs was "where they used to wash down the hearses" in the late 1800s when the building was owned by a wagon company.

"When did you first start to notice things that made you think the store might be haunted?" I asked.

"As soon as we moved in," she said. She explained that shortly after they set up shop she and her husband would notice that things seemed to have been moved around overnight. They were both certain they had locked up the night before, and no one else should have had keys. Nothing was stolen; things just weren't where they remembered them being the night before—nothing huge, just small objects. "It looked almost like someone was cleaning up," she said. Neither Lynn nor Mark could imagine anyone breaking in to clean, but they went ahead and changed the locks anyway, just to be on the safe side.

Small objects continued to get moved overnight. Then, one winter morning, Lynn discovered something far more bewildering than just a few items moved around. "The city puts salt out on the sidewalks during the winter months," she explained. "It gets on peoples' shoes and they track it in, where it gets all over the hardwood floors. Usually, we clean it up at night before we go home, but that particular evening we were just too tired to sweep up. Mark and I decided to come in a little early the next morning and clean it then. Only when we came in the next day, we found fresh footprints all through the white salty residue. They *hadn't* been there the night before, and I *know* I locked the door when we left that night," she concluded emphatically.

Lynn said she thinks the spirit may be the ghost of someone who used to work in the store; the building has been an antiques shop for many years, long before she and Mark bought the place. "She—or maybe he—is just cleaning up the way they did when they were alive and worked here." We should all have ghosts who are so helpful!

But not all the spirits who have haunted the antiques store are as benevolent as their ghostly shop assistant. When I asked Lynn what her favorite ghost story was, she had to stop and think a minute because she had seen and heard so many things in the four years she and her husband have owned her shop. "I don't know if it's my *favorite* story," she began thoughtfully, "but one of the freakiest things I ever saw happened downstairs on that yellow ramp, right after we moved in." The first floor of the shop isn't just one big room—although the main room is impressively large. However, in addition, there are a number of smaller, adjacent rooms, and one of them has a bright yellow ramp leading up to it (thus making it wheelchair accessible).

What Lynn told me she'd seen there would have been enough to make me turn around and run out the door.

"I walked in and I saw this headless guy, flailing around, right on the ramp. It was like something you'd see in a movie or something. His movements were real fast and jerky, and he looked like maybe he'd been burned."

"What did you do?"

"I just took a deep breath and waited for him to go away." Lynn told me she's found that if she doesn't pay too much attention to them, the ghosts don't usually stick around for long. I don't think I could have been so calm.

"There was a fire here," she went on to explain. "They think it was arson and that the arsonist died in the blaze. The ghost I saw was probably him." She hasn't seen him since. Many people believe that when a person dies violently, their spirit somehow gets tied to the place where they died.

Besides the headless arsonist, Lynn told me about some of the apparitions that numerous people have seen. "There's a woman that people have seen walking through a closed door downstairs," Lynn told me—and later she pointed out the door. Other customers have reported seeing a man in a top hat, dressed as if he's going out for a night on the town. Lynn told me to make sure that I checked out the "white room" when I went back downstairs, as it is also one of the more reputedly haunted areas of the shop.

One night, Lynn decided to conduct her own investigation of the shop, with the help of some friends. "We kept hearing a little girl's voice over the walkie-talkies. It definitely wasn't one of us, so at first we thought we might be picking up something from outside." Walkie-talkies can pick up radio signals pretty easily. "But then the voice started saying our names. It was pretty freaky and it convinced us that whatever we have here, it's real." Not that Lynn needed much convincing; she told me she had always believed in the paranormal.

Like many of the residents of Holly, Lynn believes that the whole village is haunted. "It's such an old town, and so many people have lived and died here," she said. She told me that she and her family had experienced a number of unusual things in their home as well and that when she started looking into the history of the shop, she discovered a connection between the house they're renting and the store. Apparently, many years ago, long before the previous owners purchased either building, both the antiques store and her home were owned by the same family.

"Is there a place in the shop that seems the most haunted?" I asked.

"Definitely up here. When customers tell me they feel like they're being watched upstairs, I usually tell them it's just the security cameras—but not all of them believe me. Some people are just more sensitive to spirits than others. We have some customers who won't even come up here anymore."

It's not just customers. Lynn told me how one of the antiques dealers who used to have a spot in the corner came to her one day and asked if she could bring a radio in. She told

Lynn that she kept hearing scratching along the floorboards and it was really unnerving. If she had music, she wouldn't have to listen to it anymore.

Lynn had no objection to the radio. When she checked the floorboards later, she couldn't find scratch marks; there wasn't any evidence of vermin, mice, or rats that might have been responsible for the scratching either.

There's another part of the upstairs that is blocked off to customers; I had thought it was just an old storage area, but Lynn told me that the ghost she saw in there unsettled her so badly that she decided to close off the room. She said he smelled strongly of tar and was wearing soiled clothing. He didn't do anything, but Lynn said she felt his presence was disturbing. Considering the things she took in stride, I was just as glad that area of her shop was blocked off.

Lynn said she thought the tar-smelling ghost might have been a railway worker because Holly was originally a railroad town. I thanked Lynn for her time and hospitality and went off to wander the shop with my husband.

SPOTLIGHT ON DUNN'S TOMB

I probably shouldn't admit to how much personal experience I have with this particular location, but I was one of those kids who visited Dunn's Tomb regularly as a teenager. My friends and I never actually did anything when we went to the old cemetery, except try to scare underclassmen with tales of mad monks and rabid German shepherds, but we probably shouldn't have been there. Truthfully, I'd forgotten about my miscreant youth until I was talking with an old friend from high school and the subject of *Ghost Hunting Michigan* came up.

"You're going to write about Dunn's Tomb, aren't you?" Frank asked. "Oh, you have to!"

He was right. I do have to write about it, not because of my own adventures, but because Dunn's Tomb is one of Oakland County's most famous allegedly haunted places. Not that I ever saw any ghosts there, or any evidence of mad monks either, although there really is a monastery nearby. Dunn's Tomb is located in the Lakeville Cemetery off of Drahner Road. The remote location is made even scarier (at least to a bunch of teenagers) by its close proximity to the Addison Oaks Country Park, a large overgrown nature preserve. The tomb has always reminded me of a burial mound more than any sort of mausoleum and is located in a remote part of the cemetery off one of the older paths. Unfortunately, that hasn't stopped vandals from frequenting the area.

There doesn't seem to be just one single story connected to Dunn's Tomb, but rather a whole collection of them. In one tale, a pair of teenagers, a boy and a girl, were dared by friends to spend the night in the old hillside mausoleum. When their friends returned the next day, the pair was dead, but there was no obvious cause of death. It is

SPOTLIGHT ON DUNN'S TOMB (CONTINUED)

said that if you happen to drive to the cemetery in a black car, you can park by the fence late at night and eventually you'll see the ghostly pair hovering nearby. Apparently, the friends who dropped them off and came to fetch them again the next morning were in a black car, and the teens are still looking for their ride home.

Another story says that visitors to the tomb return to their vehicle to find ghostly handprints on the windshield, as if someone had been touching their car, perhaps trying to get in.

In another story, a man got locked in the tomb overnight, went mad, and killed himself. In another version, rather than committing suicide, the madman became an ax murderer and kept his victims' bodies in the tomb.

None of those stories have ever been verified—and most of them are probably patently false. What is known about Dunn's Tomb is that it contains the earthly remains of James and Elizabeth Dunn. Mr. Dunn died in 1930; his wife passed away in 1952. Despite the wild stories told about the tomb, which might lead a person to discount that there's any kernel of truth hiding at the center of the legends, a number of paranormal investigators have been to the area and claim to have gotten compelling evidence that leads them to believe that someone—or something—haunts the area.

CHAPTER 7

FENTON

FENTON HOTEL TAVERN & GRILLE

Despite its name, the Fenton Hotel hasn't been an actual inn since the 1950s.

Originally constructed in 1856, the three-story brick building on the corner of Main Street and Leroy in downtown Fenton has changed hands, and names, numerous times over the last 150 years. Even so, the place retains much of its former beauty—at least on the first floor. The second and third floors are another matter. The former guest rooms have fallen into disuse, and while there is some office space upstairs most of the upper two floors are completely closed off—which doesn't stop people from swearing that sometimes they hear someone, or *something*, walking around up there. Or so the stories go.

I arrived at the Fenton Hotel on a rainy Friday night, which probably wasn't the best time to show up at a restaurant asking about their ghosts, but it was my only night that week. At that time Margaret Perry, who had been with the Fenton Hotel for nine years, greeted me at the hostess stand. She was the perfect person to talk to, but she was also extremely busy. I was grateful to her for taking a few minutes for me in between shepherding customers to their tables. One of the things I was most struck by as I watched Margaret working was how well she and the other staff members knew their customers. Over half of the guests who came in were greeted by name as staff members asked about their spouses, grandchildren, recent vacations, or fishing trips.

I had a few minutes to glance over the menu, which was classic American fare; probably if they weren't so busy, I would have stayed for dinner, but there truly wasn't a table to be had. So instead, I waited patiently by the hostess's stand for Margaret to get back to me.

"Sorry about that," she said, returning once more.

It was absolutely no problem.

After catching her breath and collecting her thoughts for a second, Margaret told me about her first encounter with the Fenton Hotel's ghostly entities. She said that when she was a new employee, she remembered standing at the hostess stand and feeling something brush against her ankles. She was pretty unnerved and started looking around, wondering if maybe a mouse had somehow gotten in, but she couldn't see anything. She kept a keen eye out but continued to see no signs of vermin.

Later on that night, one of the servers was up at the hostess stand and grumbled, "Those darned ghosts! They won't leave my ankles alone tonight!"

Perhaps it was the ghostly black cat that some believe wanders the building. Other ghosts said to inhabit the hotel-turned-tavern include a mysterious man who is occasionally observed sitting at a table in the dining room—table number 32, according to several witnesses. Even Margaret said she'd seen him once or twice.

"I was walking past that doorway there," she said, indicating the doorway between the dining room and foyer, "and thought I saw someone sitting at one of the tables, out of the corner of my eye. There shouldn't have been anyone in there—and when I blinked, he was gone."

She also told me that just the previous weekend, she came in and thought she saw a man sitting on the sofa in the foyer. She went about her business for a few minutes, and when she looked back up, the man was gone.

"It happened to me, like, three times that night. Finally, I asked my manager, 'Did you see anybody sitting in the foyer?' She said, 'No, why?' and I told her what I'd seen. She hadn't seen him." Margaret shrugged. "I guess I'm not 100% sure I saw someone; I was pretty tired that night, but. . . ." she said, her voice trailing off.

After seating a couple of customers who had come in out of the rain, Margaret told me another story.

"I was standing over by the service bar," she said—the service bar is where the wait staff orders drinks for their tables. "And I heard a man right behind me. His voice was so clear, and he said very politely 'Pardon me.' I turned around expecting to see someone trying to get past—but there was no one there."

Margaret told me about another time when she was sitting alone in the dining room eating her own dinner and saw what looked like smoke moving across the room. At first, she wondered if it was cigarette smoke, though it seemed unlikely as smoking isn't allowed in Michigan restaurants anymore.

"Then I saw what looked like lights, or orbs, in the smoke—now, the first thing I thought was that it was just light reflecting in from the window or something," she clarified. "But then I realized that it wasn't. I can't explain what I saw, but around here, there's a lot of that."

She told me, "We hear running around up on the second floor all the time."

Both guests and employees have also reported hearing a baby crying, when there weren't any children around, or that doors seem to shut all by themselves. There have been numerous reports of glasses mysteriously falling off shelves in the bar. Margaret personally witnessed a martini glass break "for no apparent reason."

"It just fell over and broke," she told me.

In fact, many people believe that the bar of the Fenton Hotel may be the most haunted part of the tavern, although other people will tell you it's the ladies' room, where many customers have reported experiencing an "eerie feeling," or even having their hair and clothing tugged on. Rumor has it that around the turn of the century, a young woman hanged herself in the hotel. She is usually described as a "working girl" who was renting one of the rooms on the hotel's third floor. The story goes that she became pregnant out of wedlock and was so distraught over her situation that she took her own life, quite possibly in the ladies restroom on the main floor. The rumor has never been substantiated, though.

While Margaret was on the phone taking a reservation, a man and woman came in. They asked me if I was waiting to be seated, but I said that no, I was writing a book about historic buildings in Michigan and that Margaret was helping me out with stories about the Fenton Hotel.

"Oh, are you writing about the ghosts?" the woman asked me.

I told her that yes, I was.

"Tell her about the time we heard that man's voice coming out of the speaker in the bar," the woman urged her companion.

He looked a little sheepish. "It was probably nothing," he said.

"We heard a man's voice singing along with the music coming out of the speakers in the bar," the woman insisted.

By then, Margaret was off the phone; apparently undeterred by their prior experiences, the couple asked for a seat in the bar if there was room.

"People certainly don't seem afraid here," I remarked to Margaret when she got back to the hostess stand.

She smiled. "No, it's just part of our charm."

Perhaps the most famous of the Fenton Hotel's ghosts is Emery, the former caretaker of the inn. Little seems to be known about Emery, other than that he once lived upstairs in a small second-floor bedroom and that he still haunts the second floor. He is the spirit who is believed to roam the second floor. He has been known to knock on the floor and walls after closing, and some staff members and customers believe he even picks up the telephone from time to time.

SPOTLIGHT ON GREENFIELD VILLAGE AND HENRY FORD MUSEUM

Many of the people I've spoken to in the course of writing this book have also said they have noticed how paranormal activity seemed to increase when they brought antiques into their businesses. So it stands to reason that a place like Dearborn's Greenfield Village and Henry Ford Museum, which is nothing but antiques and old homes, would be teeming with paranormal activity. And according to a lot of people, it is.

Greenfield Village and the Henry Ford Museum is a legacy left to us by the museum's namesake, automotive giant Henry Ford. Ford's passion for preserving American history and culture led him to amass, preserve, and exhibit more than 90 acres' worth of historically significant Americana, including large exhibits like Thomas Edison's laboratory, the Wright Brothers' bicycle shop, and many historic homes, including the Firestone Farm, which was originally constructed in 1828 in Columbiana, Ohio. Other permanent exhibits include John F. Kennedy's presidential limousine, the chair Abraham Lincoln was assassinated in, and the bus made famous by Rosa Parks. The folks who run Greenfield Village are more interested in traditional history than in paranormal activity, but several places around the village are reputed to be haunted, including the Firestone Farm, the Dagget Farm, William Ford Barn, and the Wright Brothers' home—at least according to former employees of the Village.

On the Firestone Farm, it is said that one can hear Sally Firestone walking around upstairs. Her bedroom is said to be particularly active; sometimes she can even be seen peering out the window. Former employees have reported they would find the drapes pulled back and

furniture out of place in the room. Equine specters are said to stamp their hooves in the William Ford Barn, and in the Wright Brothers' family home, people claim to have seen Katherine Wright, the famous pair's younger sister. At the Dagget Farm, some people have claimed to catch a whiff of pipe smoke, particularly in the autumn months. Most of the Village's supposedly paranormal activity happens at night, and management tends to be closed-mouthed about it. But if you ask around discretely, you might be able to get some of the employees to tell you a ghost story or two.

75
SAGINAW
BAY
Forester
LAKE
HURON
75
69
69
Memphis
75
Lansing
94
96
Lake
St Clair
94
275

THUMB AREA

ONLY
Boomers
3500

CHAPTER 8

MEMPHIS

BOOMERS TAVERN

Following a lead from some locals at a cafe in Richmond, I headed up M-19 (Main Street/Memphis Ridge Road) to the tiny little town of Memphis, Michigan, to look for a man named Mike. Although the locals, Mimi and Philip, hadn't been able to remember the name of Mike's bar, their assessment that I "wouldn't be able to miss it" was completely accurate, and within 10 minutes I was parked across the street from Boomers Tavern. Standing almost exactly at the center of downtown Memphis at the corner of Bordman Road and M-19, the big, white building looked as if it might have at one time been someone's home, or perhaps a boarding house. I parked across the street and ventured over.

I have to admit I felt a bit of trepidation as I approached; the building looked old. Really old. But my adventures had gone well thus far, so I was willing to give it a shot and walked up the front porch to try one of the doors.

"Can I help you?" called a voice.

I glanced down to see a man wearing a shirt with the name Mikey written across the pocket. I suspected that he was who I was looking for, but asked anyway.

"Hi," I greeted him with a smile. "Mimi and Philip said I should come by. They said to ask for Mike."

Just then, someone that was driving down Bordman Road slowed down and called out the window of their truck, "Hey Mike!"

Mike turned and waved to the driver, then looked back at me with an amused smile. "I'm Mike," he told me, needlessly. "What can I do for you?"

I introduced myself and explained, "I'm writing a book about haunted places in Michigan—" I didn't get any further than that, however, before he told me that I had *definitely* come to the right place if I wanted haunted.

"What do you want to know?" he asked.

Well, that was easy! I explained that I was traveling around the state visiting reputedly haunted locations, the kinds of places readers would be able to visit for themselves, and that Mimi and Philip suggested I come up to Memphis. "I'm not trying to prove or disprove anything," I cautioned. "I'm just listening to people's stories and writing them down so my readers can judge for themselves."

He laughed. "Well, I've got a few ghost stories for you, that's for sure. We've had a couple of paranormal groups come out here to investigate the place too. This is probably the oldest building in Memphis," he added. "It was originally a hotel—"

Someone else driving by called out to Mike to say hello and ask about an event going on at the tavern later that night. They talked for a couple of seconds, and then Mike turned back to me with an apologetic smile. "Sorry about that."

"I guess your customers aren't scared by the ghosts," I remarked.

"Nah, not really. Where was I?"

I reminded him that he was telling me about the history of the place. It was a subject Mike had researched diligently with the help of the Memphis Historical Society—admittedly a fairly small group, he added, but he was proud to be a part of it.

The building that is now Boomers Tavern was constructed in 1855 and was originally a stagecoach stop. During the early 1900s, it became The National Hotel, and a pretty big deal, according to Mike, who told me that it used to be a three-story building rather than the two-story structure that stands there today. I could only imagine that it must have been a big place in its day, with the main floor as a dining area, 10 guest bedrooms on the second floor, and a ballroom on the third. Unfortunately, in 1962 a fire destroyed the third story. While the guest rooms remain intact, it has been decades since the place was used as a hotel. "Although the people we bought it from in 2007 lived up on the second floor," he added.

He went on to say that the previous owner never had any unusual experiences in the building—but he described the former owner as an older fellow, so maybe he just didn't notice.

Given some of the things Mike told me he heard about the building before he bought it, I had to wonder how anyone *wouldn't* notice it—assuming the rumors were true.

"People used to claim to see 'guests' walking around upstairs or peering out of the windows on the second floor when no one was up there," Mike told me. He also said that there have been two confirmed deaths on the property, one a murder, the other someone who died of natural causes. "That was about 20 years ago and happened in one of the corner bedrooms." He pointed up to one of the windows to indicate which room.

But Mike didn't necessarily believe in the rumors himself, at least not until a series of unexplainable incidents in the bar—glasses sliding down the bar or falling off shelves and unlocked doors mysteriously locking all by themselves—made Mike begin to suspect there might be something to the ghost stories after all. Some of his bartenders, and even a few customers, also told him that every once in a while they heard what sounded like a baby crying in the bar area, but when they looked around they could see no children in the bar.

Then one day, Mike got a visit from a couple of members of ESP Michigan, a group of professional paranormal investigators who operate out of Macomb County. Like me, the members of ESP Michigan had heard about Boomers while they were in the area investigating other places and decided to check out the tavern. They talked for a while, and Mike decided to let them investigate.

"They were completely professional," he told me. "They set up their equipment in one of the upstairs bedrooms and in the bathroom." Like most old inns, there was only one bathroom upstairs, which was shared by all of the guests. He said the bathroom upstairs was one of the most active rooms in the building when it came to paranormal phenomena. "Would you like a tour of the upstairs?" Mike asked.

I was more than happy to accept, even though he warned me that upstairs wasn't in the best state. For years, it hadn't been used for anything but storage.

"Watch your step," he cautioned as we climbed the narrow back stairs off the tavern's kitchen.

Once upstairs, he showed me the communal bathroom and pointed out the room that seemed to get locked "all by itself." The room used to belong to the former owner's mother, he told me.

"We usually leave the keys in the door," he said. "It's just easier that way."

The story goes that shortly after Mike and his wife bought the building, they noticed that no matter how many times they unlocked it, they would always find a certain door locked again the next time they came up to get something or put something away.

There was another room that Mike wanted me to see too. "When the ghost hunters were here, they told me that they discovered this room used to be a nursery," he explained. "What's interesting about that is that another lady who claimed to be psychic told me the same thing."

It certainly was interesting to hear that two people who had never spoken to each other both said the room upstairs had been a nursery.

"Did either of them know the story about your staff hearing a baby crying?" I asked.

Mike said that as far as he knew, they hadn't. He told me that the ghost hunters had taken a number of photographs with orbs in them, particularly over one door. They also took video footage and captured a shadow passing in front of the camera. Supposedly, none of the team members walked in front of any of their lights; they were all standing more or less still when the shadow passed by.

Mike took me downstairs to show me some books and a calendar he had from the historical society. It was filled with old photographs of the town, including several of the bars from when it was a stagecoach stop and a three-story hotel. Mike made photocopies of some of the material for me.

He concluded my visit with one last story, as he pointed out the jukebox. "It's basically like satellite radio," he explained. "You can get just about any song you want, not like the old jukeboxes that had records in them."

I laughed—I'm just old enough to remember those.

"It was the night the ghost hunters were here," he went on. "I had a customer who was trying to get a song to play—I don't remember which one now, just that no matter what we did, it wouldn't play. I gave him his money back and it was no big deal. But that night, after we closed up—and after we turned the jukebox *off*—it suddenly turned back on again and the song the customer had been trying to play came on. There's no reason for it to have done that—other customers had played other songs after that, so it's not like it got stuck or something."

I thanked Mike for his hospitality, and then it was time for me to hit the road again.

SPOTLIGHT ON EVP (ELECTRONIC VOICE PHENOMENA)

If you visit any paranormal investigator's website, you will likely find clips of EVP recordings that were captured during the course of their investigations. I have to confess that most of the EVP recordings I've listened to sound like either white noise or garbled nonsense. The human mind is very susceptible to suggestion. Just like we often see what we want to see, we also frequently hear what we want to hear. But every once in a while I run across an EVP recording that makes me doubt my own skepticism, because it sounds so clear and the words spoken are so distinct. Of course, this could be because the recording device is picking up a radio station or even CB (citizens band radio) chatter—except that quite frequently the recorded voices are responding to questions or even calling investigators by name. What is interesting about these recordings is that the ghostly responses can only be heard on the tape; they aren't detectable by human ears otherwise.

For as long as there have been audio recording devices, there have been people attempting to record the voices of the dead. Even Thomas Edison is said to have attempted to make contact with the spirit world in the 1890s—he wasn't successful. The first known EVP recording wasn't captured until 1938; the recording was made with a phonograph (an early record player).

But it was Friedrich Jergenson (1903–1987) who truly pioneered the study of electronic voice phenomena. The story says that he was recording bird songs and when he played the recording back, he realized there were human voices in the background. Jergenson didn't recall having heard any people where he was recording. His curiosity

aroused, he began making "recordings of nothing," simply setting up his equipment in quiet places, with no other people around to see what he could capture on tape. Ultimately, he claimed to have recorded the voice of his own long-dead mother and came to believe that somehow he was recording voices from beyond the grave. Many researchers have followed after Jergenson, attempting to both prove and disprove his theories.

Almost any recording device can be used to record EVPs; although these days, digital recorders are probably the most popular. They're small, inexpensive, and have greater recording times than audiocassettes. The important thing is to have a sensitive microphone, because often ghostly voices caught on tape are hushed whispers. Many paranormal investigators suggest using an external microphone rather than relying on the microphone built into your recorder.

The technique most often employed by investigators is to begin by asking any ghosts in the area to talk to you. You might then ask a series of questions, such as "What is your name?" "Where are you from?" and "Why are you here?" Pause after each question to give the spirits the opportunity to respond. When you're done, you can play back the recording to see if you've captured anything that sounds like an answer. Experts say the best EVP recordings are the ones that sound like real human voices.

Another method of gathering audio evidence of supernatural activity is to do like I did at the Blue Pelican Inn and simply leave your recorder on all night—but that can make for some very boring listening the next day!

FORESTER
TOWNSHIP
CEMETERY

CHAPTER 9

FORESTER

FORESTER TOWNSHIP CEMETERY

I had been reluctant to write about cemeteries, even though it's where one would think looking for ghost stories would be the easiest. But part of my job—in fact, the part I love the most—in writing this book is talking to people. Hearing their ghost stories. It's hard to do that in a cemetery. Lighthouses, restaurants, and theaters all have employees I can talk to. With a cemetery, it is a lot harder to find an employee on duty. Besides, a good deal of the activity that allegedly takes place at cemeteries happens after dark, which in most cases is when cemeteries are closed to the public.

The next place I visited was the Crimson and Clover florist shop. I explained to the young woman behind the counter that I had been sent down because there was a chance she or her coworkers had experienced some of the same unusual happenings that the employees of the Main Street Café used to before the business was sold.

She had . . . but she wasn't comfortable talking about it in any detail; I should really ask her boss but she was off for the weekend. We exchanged business cards, and we talked for a couple of minutes, because, once again, I had run into someone who was interested in the project I was working on.

"Do you know the story of Minnie Quay?" she asked me.

No, I hadn't heard it, but that was probably because I wasn't really investigating people; I was looking into haunted places. Of course, that didn't

Gifts left by visitors to the Quay/Shaw tombstone at Forester Cemetery

mean I wasn't eager to hear what the woman in the florist shop had to tell me. Some of the best leads can be garnered just by talking to people.

"Me and my friends visit Minnie Quay's grave every time we drive out to Caseville," the young woman at the florist shop told me. "A lot of people do. You're supposed to go and leave something for her, like a token, because her story is so sad. She was in love with a sailor who died in a shipwreck and it broke her heart so much that she walked into Lake Huron and drowned. Lots of people have seen her ghost walking along the shore," she added.

That story sparked my interest enough that after I checked into a motel for the night, I booted up my laptop and did some digging. It wasn't long before I was figuring out the best way to work the Forester Township Cemetery into my trip.

Forester is an unincorporated township on Lake Huron's coast, located about 60 miles north of Port Huron. And it is truly little more than a dot on the map. With a population of barely over a thousand people spread out over 25 square miles (very little of it built up in any significant way), the first thing I discovered when I arrived at Forester Township Cemetery was that the address I found online for the cemetery does not correspond with its actual location. Fortunately, it wasn't off by more than a few hundred feet, and the cemetery itself wasn't difficult to find, so even though my GPS told me to keep driving, I turned into the little graveyard anyway. Once I parked, the search for the Quay family plot began. I was more than grateful that the Forester Township Cemetery wasn't especially large. The headstone I eventually found, marked Quay/Shaw, seemed to be a different stone from the one I had seen a photo of online—but there was plenty of evidence of visitors leaving tokens for Minnie. I figured that even if I didn't have the "right" Quay gravesite, I at least was at one that was visited by people who had wished to pay their respects to the lovelorn young woman.

The Quay/Shaw headstone I visited is off the southern road into the cemetery, about halfway to the back. The headstone faces the back of the cemetery, perhaps intentionally, as the cemetery overlooks Lake Huron. Later, I found out that "Shaw" is the name of the last descendants of the Quay family, so it could be that I had been in the right place after all and that the headstone had simply been updated.

Unlike a lot of other urban legends, especially those attached to cemeteries—and *especially* those you find online—the facts of Minnie Quay's story are true. She was born in 1861 and lived in Forester with her parents, Mary Ann and James, and a younger brother. Although Forester doesn't look like much now, when the Quay family was living, it was, like so many other little towns in Michigan, a city booming with industry and commerce. As a result, freighters and their crews were frequently coming and going through town. Unfortunately, sailors have never enjoyed a very good reputation, and when Minnie Quay, a young woman of 15 or 16 (accounts vary) fell in love with one, her parents were not happy. No information seems to be recorded about the young man, so it is impossible to say whether or not his intentions were noble or, as the Quays no doubt feared, he had a girl in every port. All that is known is that James and Mary Ann forbid their daughter to continue the affair. When Minnie refused to break it off, her parents forcibly moved the girl out of her own room into a small bedroom adjacent to their own, probably originally a nursery. The next time Minnie's young sailor came into town, James and Mary Ann locked their daughter in that room and refused to let her out until he was gone.

In early spring of 1876, word reached Minnie that the ship her lover had been on was caught in a storm on the lake and sank. All hands on board were drowned. Minnie's grief was doubled because not only was her lover dead, but her parents had prevented her from seeing him the last time he was in town. Had she been allowed to see him, she would at least have been able to say goodbye before what would be his last voyage.

On May 26, 1876, Minnie's parents left her in charge of her younger brother while they went out to run errands. Shortly after James and Mary Ann left the house, Minnie put her brother down for a nap and walked down to the lake, wearing a white gown, according to eyewitnesses. She walked to Forester Pier, just past the Tanner House hotel where bystanders watched in shock and horror as she jumped to her death off the end of the pier into Lake Huron.

Her restless spirit is said to wander along the shore near the remains of Forester Pier at night, and many people claim to have seen her, including several people I talked to when I stopped for gas just outside of town. The stories were all pretty much the same: someone walking along the beach near Forester

Pier at night would spot a figure off in the distance and assume it was someone else out for a stroll until they looked back and the other person wasn't there anymore. Locals believe that Minnie was never reunited with her sailor, even in death, which is why she still haunts the beach where she drowned. Her ghost has also allegedly been spotted around the old Tanner House hotel, which still stands and is located at the corner of M-25 and Forester Road.

Minnie's story was so moving to talented Michigander Jory Brown that he wrote a folk ballad entitled "The Ghost of Minnie Quay." Whether you believe in ghosts or not, Minnie Quay's story is certainly a tragic one.

LAKE MICHIGAN
Grand Haven
96
31
131
96
196
Allegan
69
Kalamazoo
94
Portage
Marshall
131
94

WESTERN MICHIGAN

CHAPTER 10

KALAMAZOO

HENDERSON CASTLE

I was headed to Kalamazoo on a completely unrelated errand, but I couldn't resist the urge to type "haunted places in Kalamazoo" into my favorite Internet search engine the night before I left. The first place to come up was Henderson Castle. As soon as I saw a picture of the place, I knew I wanted to visit! I didn't even know exactly what the castle was, I just knew it was open to the public and spectacularly beautiful. I'm a huge fan of Victorian architecture—I love old buildings in general, but Victorian-era houses are my favorite. The next question, of course, was "Is it really haunted?" Experience has taught me that you can't believe everything you read online.

I did a little more digging, and I came up with a news article confirming that there really were reports of ghostly activity at Henderson Castle and that the building had been visited by at least one paranormal investigation team, the Southern Michigan ParaNormals. They've been out to Henderson Castle several times over the years and have collected a good bit of evidence, mostly in the form of EVPs (electronic voice phenomena) and personal experiences, to support the claims that the ghosts of Mr. and Mrs. Frank Henderson, who built the castle in 1895, are still "in residence."

There are several other spirits who seem to haunt the castle, including several children, probably little girls. They have been heard by both staff and guests, laughing in the halls—or so the story goes.

The castle—and, truly, Henderson Castle deserves the name "castle"—was originally a private home. But more than building his dream home, Frank Henderson had a hand in shaping the entire subdivision in which his castle resides. Sadly, however, Mr. Henderson only got to live in his dream house for four years. He passed away in 1899 and was buried in the cemetery across the street. His grave is on a hill, overlooking the castle. His wife, Mary, remained in their home for another nine years before moving away. The castle changed hands several times over the next few years, with each owner making his or her own changes.

Henderson Castle is reported to have cost $72,000 when it was built over 100 years ago. There are 25 rooms, including seven baths, a sauna, and a ballroom on the third floor. Supposedly, a number of "secret passageways" are hidden throughout the house. I suspected as I was reading the articles that these were really just back halls intended for servants' use and not really secret passageways at all.

A much later addition to the castle was a rooftop hot tub, which seems in keeping with Henderson's goal of building a home that, according to the castle's website, "exemplified the most expensive tastes of the time."

In the 1920s, the carriage house was converted into a garage, but that has since been turned into a separate residence. Later, in 1945, the main house was divided into apartments—and it must have been a magnificent place to live. Eventually, the castle became a part of Kalamazoo College but then was sold back into private ownership when Dr. Jess Walker purchased it in 1975. Dr. Walker began the arduous task of restoring the property; the task was taken over in 1981 by Fred Royce, who continued the job of restoring the castle and eventually turned it into a bed-and-breakfast. I was more than pleasantly surprised to discover that the room rates for an overnight stay at Henderson Castle are competitive with other bed-and-breakfasts (about the same as a three- or four-star hotel)—but I was really only planning a day trip. Maybe next time I have to head up that way, I'll stay overnight.

I printed my directions and finished getting my gear together for my road trip to Kalamazoo. I tossed an extra set of AAs into my bag in case any mischievous ghosts (or my teenager) decided to get hold of my camera and drain the batteries. After my visit to the Baldwin Theatre, I learned my lesson. Once I had everything set, it was off to bed early; I wanted to get up and on the road early to avoid the morning rush hour.

Kalamazoo proved to be about a three-hour drive from my metro Detroit home—MapQuest had insisted it would only take 2 hours. They took me on four highways where I normally would have only taken two, I-75 and I-94. Lesson learned: next time I'll read over the directions *before* hitting the road. It was probably a good thing I'd left my husband at home that day. He no doubt would have laughed at me—and he really doesn't have my passion for old houses or ghost stories.

It was a gorgeous day for a drive. I had the windows rolled down and the music turned up. I was excited about the trip in part because I hadn't been to Kalamazoo since I was in high school. In my senior year, we took a field trip to Western Michigan University for a marching band competition. Being there with 60 classmates and half a dozen chaperones prevented me from seeing much of the city, but I remember wishing I'd had more time for sightseeing. So I was looking forward to playing tourist, albeit a tourist on a mission. In addition to Henderson Castle, there were three other places I wanted to visit. This time around, I hadn't made any appointments; I was just dropping in and hoping for the best.

Over the past few months, I'd discovered that there wasn't any real secret to getting people to talk to me about their ghost stories, other than simply asking nicely. Some people have been amenable to being interviewed and happy to show me around, while employees at other venues are more reluctant. Only two, so far, have flat-out asked me not to even mention their property at all. A couple of the places I've visited have required more than one trip to talk to the resident "expert" on the venue's ghosts, but I've had about the same success just "dropping in" as I've had when I'd tried to make an appointment. So as soon as I finished up my other errands, I headed to Kalamazoo's west side and Henderson Castle.

Kalamazoo's roads are a bit on the twisty side, but I only got lost once—Academe Street isn't clearly labeled on one side of the road. Once I found it, however, it was only a couple more turns before I discovered that pictures truly do not do Henderson Castle justice. Not only did it sit atop a very high hill, just like a real castle, but it was *so* much bigger in person than it looked online! For the first time since I'd started working on this project, I felt a little intimidated as I walked toward the front steps and up onto the huge, wrap-around porch. Was my slip showing? Was my hair still neat in its braid, or had a million little wisps flown loose like always?

Finding the front door open, I stepped quietly inside and found myself surrounded by polished wood, white marble, and gleaming brass. Classical music filled the foyer, and off to my left, I saw the dining room. The tables were set with black cloths; it looked very regal.

No one seemed to be around to greet me, so I ventured further inside. Bed-and-breakfast inns are often also the proprietors' homes, and while most B&B owners welcome guests, they also have a business to run.

Finally, I spied an open door and a man in a chef's coat and jeans working at his computer. His back was to me, so I announced myself by saying, "Good morning."

He turned and greeted me with a welcoming smile. "Good morning, how are you today?"

Bolstered by the warmth of the chef's "hello," I held out my hand and introduced myself, hoping that even if the management of Henderson Castle didn't want their inn to end up in a book about ghosts, they might at least let me look around the grounds. I'm sure I sounded nervous as I explained the reason for my visit, but he just kept smiling. When I stopped to take a breath, he asked a few questions and said that he was François. I realized he must be the owner, François Moyet, who had taken over Henderson Castle in August of 2011. He was also willing to give me a few minutes of his time.

"This place is . . . I'm not sure if I would say *haunted,*" François began, a little bit cautiously, "but we seem to have some interesting positive activity going on." He stressed that whatever was in the castle, it was definitely a benevolent entity that was looking out for him and his staff. "Most people say it's Mr. Henderson," he told me. "He wanted to be buried in the cemetery across the street. He's on the hill, so he can still see his house."

I suppose if I'd built my dream house and only gotten to live in it for a few years, I might want to keep an eye on it from the afterlife too.

François went on, "Personally, the only thing I really witnessed here . . . well, let me show you." He led the way toward the dining room. The room is lit by wall sconces—all electric, of course, but otherwise what you'd expect to see in a Victorian home (Victorians would have used gas to fuel their lights). François explained that although the lights each had individual on-off switches, they were all wired to a main switch at the doorway. That way, all he or someone else had to do was flip one switch to light up the entire room.

"It was the night of Halloween," he explained, "and I came in to turn the lights on. I flipped the switch, and nothing happened. At first, I thought maybe we blew a fuse, but the fuses were all okay. So I came back up and walked over to the light." He walked me over to demonstrate—the switches on the sconces themselves are tiny knobs that look more decorative than functional. "I tried the switch. The light came on. If it had just been one, I might have not thought anything of it, but every single sconce was turned off at the switch, at the light itself." He felt certain that no member of his staff or any of the guests were responsible.

"I've felt some activity," he added, "whenever I've brought in new furniture."

All of the furnishings in the castle appeared to be antiques, and I remembered what I had learned on past trips: Spirits seem to become attached to things that belonged to them in life, especially dolls, mirrors, and larger items, like furniture. François speculated that perhaps if any spirits had been attached to the antiques he brought, those "spirits might be fighting amongst themselves"—but not in any sort of negative way that disturbed the castle's living inhabitants. François felt that perhaps Mr. Henderson doesn't mind people so much but is less tolerant of other spirits coming into his home.

François also had a number of secondhand stories to tell me. An employee told him that a number of years ago, a spiritualist medium working with the FBI on a cold case visited Henderson Castle. While at the castle, the medium offered to do a reading to see if she could get in touch with any spirits who might be there. The owners agreed and the medium was able to contact Mr. Henderson. She said that Mr. Henderson told her he was very upset with a 4-year-old child he called "little Christine" because she had written something on the ceiling. That was as much information as she was able to get, however.

Perplexed by the tale, François called Fred Royce, the former owner, to ask if he knew anything about "little Christine" or writing on the ceiling. Fred told François that, yes, there *had* been some writing on the ceiling that they found when he was renovating. "Fred told me that they tried to remove it, sand it, revarnish it, but the writing always came back."

But that wasn't the end of the story. Two months ago, François told me that a paranormal investigation team visited him. One of the women told him that she had visited the castle when she was a little girl and that she had a "secret friend" there who played with her—a 4-year-old girl named Christine.

"So there you have two independent stories with Christine," said François. I had to admit, I was becoming convinced myself that there might be something to the story.

"And then," François told me, "in December or January, during a Murder Mystery weekend, one of the guests came to me to show me a photograph she'd taken on the stairs. There was a shape in it." He pointed to the wide staircase leading up to the second floor. Over the stairs is a huge stained glass window. "I looked at the photo and thought, 'That's Mr. Henderson!'" François explained that the apparition was very clear and looked just like the portrait he'd seen of Mr. Henderson in the basement. The guest assured him that when she took the picture, there was no one standing there.

Stained glass window in front of which a guest took a picture of Mr. Henderson's ghost

François ended our conversation by reaffirming that whatever spiritual activity he has got in the castle is "very positive," and he feels that Mr. Henderson's spirit has been a great beneficial influence on the property.

I asked if it was all right to have a look around. François welcomed me to go into any of the open rooms and walk around.

THE NATIONAL HOUSE INN
Bed & Breakfast

CHAPTER 11

MARSHALL

THE NATIONAL HOUSE INN

Sitting right in the middle of Marshall, on the southwest corner of the traffic circle surrounding the beautiful Brooks Memorial Fountain, is the oldest operating bed-and-breakfast in Michigan. Built in 1835 by Colonel Andrew Mann, The National House Inn is the oldest brick building in the United States and the oldest business in the Marshall/Battle Creek area. It is also believed to have been a stop on the Underground Railroad.

During its first few decades, the quaint inn went through changes of ownership and several names, until it finally had to close its doors in 1878. At that time, it was converted into a factory. Then, in 1902, the building was purchased by a local veterinarian who remodeled the building into eight luxury apartments. "Dean's Flats," as it was known at the time, survived into the latter half of the 20th century, but like so many other old buildings, it eventually fell into disrepair. In 1976, Norm and Kathryn Kinney came to the rescue of the old building and offered to restore the inn to its original purpose. It was a huge and largely volunteer effort, but on Thanksgiving Day of that same year, The National House Inn officially opened for business.

With such a long and varied history, it's little wonder there have been stories circulating on the Internet for years about it being haunted.

When I arrived, innkeeper Barb Bradley greeted me with a warm smile and welcoming "hello." Barb worked at the inn since 1982 and had been an owner since 1994, so if anyone would have known whether or not there was any truth to the rumor of the building being haunted, it was Barb.

I explained the reason for my visit, and she nodded, telling me that, yes, every once in a while, someone asked about the inn's supposed ghosts. She invited me to sit down with her in the dining room, just off the foyer. The dining room was reminiscent of a cozy country kitchen, so I was surprised later when she said that sometimes they seat as many as 30 guests there. It wasn't that it wasn't a big room, it just felt more like sitting down in a favorite relative's kitchen than a hotel dining room.

"My take on our ghost stories is pretty lighthearted," Barb told me. "But that's just me; I'm a lighthearted person. And the truth is that I've never believed in ghosts or even been interested, or anything like that. I know that might seem a little unusual," she added with a smile. "Running an old building like this, it seems like some people just assume I'm also interested in the ghosts that seem to go hand in hand with places like this, but I'm not. What I love is running the inn, entertaining guests, making them feel welcome. For me it's all about the inn, the restoration and preservation of the building, and creating a comfortable, beautiful place for guests to come and enjoy our little town. Of course," she added with a smile, "that doesn't mean I don't *hear* ghost stories from our guests. I'm just not sure I believe in them."

I assured Barb that I wasn't out to prove or disprove anything or to change anybody's mind one way or the other about what they believed. I was just interested in the stories she'd heard over the years.

"Probably the most famous story is the one about the lady in the red dress," she began. She also assured me that it was completely fabricated. "There are some other stories that might be true, but the lady in the red dress is just a local legend. Anyway, the story goes that there was this woman . . . a prostitute who used to work in the area, back when the house was really run down. Nobody is exactly sure when that was; the house was in sad shape for a long time. But, anyway, the story is that this woman died here. People who believe the legend think she still haunts the building. What I think is that maybe because they believe it, their minds are open to it. So, if someone sees something out of the corner of their eye or maybe catches a glimpse of something out the window that looks like it might be red, they think it must be the lady in red. But I can tell you that I've been here for more than 20 years, and I've never seen her."

But what Barb *told* me about the inn was far more interesting than an old urban legend.

"When I first started here—I think I'd been here for less than a week—my boss, a really wonderful man named Steven Poole, came to me and said that there was a group coming up to the inn from the University of Michigan. They were going to hold a séance here in the parlor, and did I want to join them? She went wide-eyed at the memory, although she was laughing too. "Well, I didn't know what to say except 'no.' I could hardly believe anyone would ask something like that. Steven told me that I wasn't the only one—he'd asked all the staff, and hardly anyone wanted to be a part of it."

"I'm not sure I blame you," I told her.

"Well, the next day Steven was really nervous even talking about what had happened here the night before. He said it was *so real* and that the things he witnessed didn't have any kind of logical explanation. I really wish I would have been here, just to see what had him so unnerved. The one story he did tell me was that these people who came up from the University of Michigan to study the house told him that there were two people—spirits, I guess—in the house. It's an older couple and they 'live' upstairs in the Dickey Room. They're very peaceful," she said. "But they're very much there. That makes that room the most haunted room in the house. When I have guests who call wanting to rent a room for the night because of the spirits who are supposed to 'live' here, that's always the room they ask for."

Barb also said that the investigators from the university told her former boss that a death had taken place in the house, at the top of the back staircase. The investigators claimed to have felt the spirit of someone who had been murdered there but weren't able to be any more specific than that. Given the house's long history, it seemed unlikely that they would be able to confirm the report.

"Those are probably the strongest stories—but there is one other that was quite moving. It was the middle of a really busy breakfast, the dining room was full, and this couple who had been staying with us for a few days came downstairs, all bundled up in their coats. It was winter," she explained. "They were ready to check out, but they didn't want to leave until they had a private word with me. I was sure that something must be wrong, maybe something had happened with the plumbing or a light fixture or . . . something. What I wasn't prepared to hear was that they had been in touch with this spirit, this little ghost boy named Jason, all during their stay. They said he was all alone because nobody else could see him, so he had no one to talk to, and that he'd been there since the late 1800s. They said that they would be back when they could, but in the meantime, could I please talk to Jason, so he wouldn't be so lonely? I didn't know quite what to say to that," she confessed.

I'm not sure I would have known what to say to that either.

Barb said she handled it as gracefully as she could by saying something to the effect that since she wasn't the person who had received the message, maybe she wasn't the best person to ask. "That was over 13 years ago, but I still remember it like it was yesterday," she told me. "They were so sincere, and it was *so* real for them. Because it was about a child, I couldn't help but feel moved too, but just didn't know what to do with it."

Over the years several paranormal groups have investigated the inn and have come up with evidence of activity. Barb's favorite "investigators" were a couple of young boys who used to come around the outside of the inn during the 1980s. "It was right after the movie *Ghostbusters* came out. These little guys would dress up in their coveralls and they had little props—and they were very polite," she added. "They never bothered us or the guests or asked to come inside. They would just walk around the outside of the property looking for ghosts." We both laughed.

Before I left, Barb showed me around the rest of the inn, taking me upstairs and letting me have a look at some of the bedrooms. The National House Inn is truly a lovely place and Barb made my visit sweet.

Marshall was named by the National Trust of Historic Preservation as one of their "Dozen Distinctive Destinations"—not just for Michigan but for the entire country. Marshall is definitely one of the most beautiful cities in Michigan, full of gorgeous 19th-century architecture and rich cultural history—*and* there's a walking tour of haunted buildings that includes private homes.

You can bet that when I go back to Marshall for another visit, I'll be indulging both my love of things that go bump in the night *and* my love of old buildings.

REGENT
THEATRE
THE ARTIST
PG13
THE OLD REGENT THEATRE CO.
"NOW SHOWING
7 DAYS A WEEK."

CHAPTER 12

ALLEGAN

REGENT THEATRE

We've all heard the expression, "Persistence pays off," but never were those words so true for me than the day I returned to the western side of Michigan. Although I stopped in at a couple of interesting places the day I visited Kalamazoo and Henderson Castle, my other errands prevented me from doing much more than making a few cursory inquiries. One of the places I stopped at was Stuart Manor in Portage, near Kalamazoo. Unfortunately, I was never able to meet the woman I hoped to speak with. I was a little disappointed, but I had a pretty long list of places to visit over the two days I'd set aside for exploring, so I hit the highway again and traveled to the next stop on my list.

Not only did I strike out at my next stop, but also the stop after that didn't yield any interesting stories either. I was seriously thinking about packing it in and going home to my husband and dog, but as I looked at my map, I thought, "I'm here anyway, so I might as well try *one* more stop. Allegan is only half an hour up the road. If there's nothing there, I'll grab a hotel for the night and head home in the morning."

When I called my husband to check in later, I exclaimed that I'd hit pay dirt and told him he wouldn't see me until the next afternoon, at the earliest; I had a lot of ground to cover.

Allegan is a quiet little town that straddles the Kalamazoo River, about 30 miles north and west of Kalamazoo. My destination was in the heart of Allegan's historic district—none of the homes and buildings I passed looked younger than a hundred years old. I arrived around 6:30 p.m.—perfect timing for my visit to the Regent Theatre, an old cinema house that wouldn't open its doors until 7 p.m. There was practically no traffic on the streets of Allegan, and about half the shops were already closed up for the day.

I had little difficulty finding a parking spot (although the one-way streets were a little tricky) and took some time to walk around. If nothing else, I was at least getting some really great photographs of beautiful old buildings. One of the most striking was the Regent itself.

Originally built in the late 1800s as a livery stable, the Regent Theatre has gone through numerous renovations and reinventions over the past century, starting in 1902 when the stable was converted into a Buick garage. It wasn't until 1919 that the building was used as a theater, initially for vaudeville. Then, in the 1930s, the Regent was redecorated in the popular Art Deco style and reopened as a silent movie house. Much like the Baldwin, which I had toured earlier in the month, the Regent was eventually converted to "talkies"—but fell into disuse in the 1980s. Within a decade, it was slated for demolition and would most likely not be standing were it not for the efforts of the Old Regent Theatre Company, which purchased the property in 1990. The nonprofit organization, comprised mainly of volunteers, rescued the once-beautiful old building and began the monumental task of renovation. The plan was to restore the theater to the way it had looked in the 1930s. The operation took six years, and in 1996 the Regent, which now shows first-run movies, had its grand reopening.

During these renovations, the ghosts who haunt the theater were "woken up" or somehow provoked into making themselves known. Pretty much everyone I talked to while writing this book indicated that spirits don't like change. I guess some people are as stubborn in death as they are in life. The Regent has been the subject of several paranormal investigations and has been visited by both the West Michigan Ghost Hunter's Society and the Ghost Research Society. The West Michigan Ghost Hunter's Society took several photographs of orbs in the lobby of the Regent.

There have been reports of cold spots and a generally "eerie feeling" throughout the building—but most of the evidence I found online was a bit scant, so I was hoping to find someone who could tell me more. I approached the lobby with a sense of nostalgia—the Regent reminded me a lot of the little movie house we used to go to when I was a kid. Stepping into the lobby foyer felt very much like taking a step back in time. I made my way over to the ticket booth and was greeted with a warm smile. Apparently, I was the first customer of the night.

I explained that I wasn't really there to see a movie, I was writing a book on haunted places in Michigan, and the Regent had come up in my research.

"We're haunted, all right," said the young woman in the ticket booth. "Hang on a minute, let me get Alicia, she's our manager. She can tell you more than I can."

While I waited patiently for the manager to come down, I had a look around the lobby, where a number of newspaper articles detailing the theater's history were on display. From one of them, I learned that while there were several paid employees—all local teenagers—all of the adults on staff were volunteers. I also discovered that despite its antiquated appearance, the Regent shows only first-run movies—admittedly, only one at a time. I also couldn't help but notice that the prices at the concession stand were at least 50% less than in any cinema I'd been to in a very long time.

Presently, a young woman in blue jeans and a T-shirt came down the stairs and introduced herself as Alicia. She apologized for keeping me waiting and asked how she could help with my book.

Projection booth window

"I'm travelling around Michigan talking to people who work in reputedly haunted places," I told her. "And was wondering if you've ever experienced anything unusual or had anyone tell you about anything unusual."

"I know a guy supposedly had a heart attack in the projection booth. I don't know if it's true or not, but some people have claimed to see a shadowy figure up there," Alicia told me. "I've had people tell me about cold spots or feeling uncomfortable—stuff like that. Sometimes you see things out of the corner of your eye, like a shadow moving, or you just feel like somebody's watching you, or get a weird feeling. In April, the Grand Rapids Paranormal Investigation team is supposed to come out and do a full investigation. It'll be interesting to hear what they find. We're a pretty old building, so it's hard to say if it's haunted or just drafty. Sometimes lights flicker, but that's probably just the wiring."

We talked a little bit about the age of the building and its history for a while, and I learned that a year after its grand reopening, the Regent's roof collapsed. Luckily, no one was hurt, but it was a major setback for the theater. Alicia showed me a picture of the damage—there was a lot of it.

"We had to replace all the seats downstairs, but the ones in the balcony are really cool because they're so old," Alicia told me. I was considering staying for the movie, but then Alicia told me that if I wanted to talk to someone who might know more than she did, I should go across the street; she'd just seen Fred step back into his shop. "His family used to own the theater," she explained.

I thanked Alicia for her time and hurried across the street to the shop she had indicated the B and C Emporium. The door was locked and the sign flipped to "closed," but I could see the owner near the back, so I knocked. A moment later, Fred opened the door and welcomed me in. I apologized for showing up when he was trying to close and explained Alicia had sent me over in the hopes that I could get some more information about the Regent Theatre's history and its ghosts.

"It's not just the theater—the whole town is haunted," Fred informed me. "There's the ghost dogs that come around after dark. Sometimes they look just like regular dogs, other times you only see part of the dog, just the front half. There used to be a breeder in town," he explained. "And then there's the site of the old Yellow Motel and the Allegan Grill and the Elks Lodge. And I have pictures I've taken myself inside the Griswold Theatre with huge orbs in them," he held his hands apart to demonstrate the size. "I took the pictures myself," he repeated, "so I *know* what's on them, that nobody went in and tampered with it."

Wow. Okay, that's a lot of ghost stories. I asked him if he knew anything about the Regent's ghost.

"Well, we've had several groups out to investigate the Regent Theatre, and I've personally seen the old manager looking out that window there." He pointed to a little window over the theater's neon sign. "That's the projection booth," he said. "The manager died some years ago," he added, "but he's still around." He went on to explain that the manager had been a friend of his family, so, no, he wasn't at all spooked to see him still watching out over the theater. Fred told me that he's heard knocking around in his own shop from time to time, when there's no one around. He's checked for raccoons and other vermin but has not seen evidence that they might be responsible for the noises that periodically come from his upstairs.

"You know that Al Capone used to visit Allegan, don't you?" Fred asked me.

No, I hadn't known that, but I was intrigued.

"Oh yeah. They say he stayed at the Yellow Motel." He shrugged. "There's no proof, but lots of rumors, guys showing up in black cars in the middle of the night, that kind of thing. Some people say there are bodies buried on the grounds of the Yellow Motel." He shrugged again and told me that if I wanted to know more, I could look it up pretty easily online after I settled in for the night. He also told me about his friend, fellow Allegan resident Kass Hillard, who conducts "ghost walks" through town around Halloween. She's the cofounder of Michigan Paranormal Encounters and has organized a number of paranormal events in town.

Before we parted company, Fred gave me directions to the Griswold, which is just a few blocks from the Regent. No one was around, but the library was right next door, so I stopped in and talked to one of the librarians for a little while. She was very helpful, and I took a few hours to do some research before heading off to find a hotel for the night.

I discovered some pretty wild stories regarding both the living and the dead, as well as their activities at the Yellow Motel and in the surrounding woods. Several reputable sources did note that Al Capone spent time in western Michigan in the 1920s and may well have visited Allegan, which is only about 150 miles from Chicago. Capone moved to Chicago in the early 1920s and is only one of the city's less-than-reputable citizens to have visited western Michigan.

The Yellow Motel is no longer standing, but some of the other places Fred told me about are still around and open to the public—although some, like the Griswold Auditorium, don't keep any sort of regular hours. It was dusk when I left the library, and I took a walk along the waterfront plaza downtown, hoping to catch a glimpse of some ghost dogs, but while plenty of ordinary canines marked my passing by barking at me, there were no ghosts to be seen that night. Just the same, I've decided to come back to Allegan again sometime, as I've completely fallen in love with the town.

GRILL HOUSE

CHAPTER 13

ALLEGAN

GRILL HOUSE RESTAURANT

Before leaving Allegan, I decided to swing by the Grill House Restaurant. If I'd paid closer attention to the menu online before heading out, I probably would have skipped my fast-food lunch. But I had a lot of ground to cover before heading home that night, and I didn't want to stop for a meal, even though the Grill House was only about a 10-minute drive from the motel where I had stopped for the night—a decidedly not-haunted Budget Host.

Afterword, when I was researching the Grill House's history, I discovered that they have been featured on the Travel Channel's program *Food Paradise*. After I finally had the chance to peruse their menu, I could see why. The main menu features items like kettle chip nachos, calamari, and a "meal splitter special," where two people get to split an entrée, but each receives a full serving of side dishes.

The next time I'm in the neighborhood, I think I'm going to stop in for a "basket of scraps"—hand-cut steak, breaded and served with a dipping sauce. If I manage to drag my husband with me, we may have to come after 4:30 p.m., when the grill is ready, because the Grill House features something unique I'd never heard of before: a grill-your-own-steak option. Expert grill masters are on hand to coach customers through the experience—not that my husband would need the help; he's a chef, but he'd probably have a lot of fun. Apparently, these grill-your-own-steak style restaurants are much more popular in Iowa, where Grill House owner Marcia Wagner grew up. Customers can even order butcher-shop quality meat to take home with them.

Originally known as the Hubbard House, the huge, old farmhouse was built in 1836 by Samuel Hubbard, a Massachusetts Supreme Court judge. Hubbard was one of the driving forces behind the settlement of the village of Allegan and built the farmhouse as a boardinghouse for lumberjacks who were coming into the area looking for work in the newly established town. The Hubbard House was the very first public lodging and saloon built in Allegan.

Marcia and her husband Dan, purchased the property in 1998 and made several renovations. Firm believers in "shopping locally," the Wagners ran into an unusual problem in 2003 when they were helping their daughter plan her wedding. There wasn't a venue in town large enough to host the event—so they built one! The Silo banquet hall stands where the old barn used to stand, just behind the Grill House, and is described on the hall's website as "a Grand Ballroom that exemplifies elegance in the country."

I pulled into the parking lot just a few minutes before the restaurant opened at 11:00 a.m. The huge, old building looked very much like the farmhouse it used to be, complete with a large front porch—although the entrance was actually off to the side, adjacent to the parking lot. The door was unlocked, so I ventured inside where I found a young man mopping the stairs that led up to the main dining room. I explained the reason for my visit, and he told me to go on up and ask for Brian. I headed toward the bar and was immediately taken by the Grill House's elegant décor. Rather than a rustic farmhouse, the interior of the Grill House reminded me of an upscale restaurant, with antiques (or at least replicas), white table cloths, and pastel-painted walls—however, the casual attire and warm greeting of the wait staff made me feel completely "at home." It seemed to me as if the Wagners definitely got it right when they called their restaurant "elegance in the country."

The waitresses smiled when I explained why I was there. They told me "Yes, the place is definitely haunted, and, yes, Brian is who you want to talk to." They offered me a seat and something to drink while I waited for Brian to come down from the office.

I learned that Brian was not only the manager but also the Wagners' nephew, and that he had lived on-site for a while, moving into the living quarters upstairs with his aunt and uncle to help them run the place. He was very gracious about talking to me and moved us over to a table in a closed section of the dining room where it was quieter. Brian asked me if I was familiar with the legend of the Grill House's ghost, "Jack," and I had to confess that I wasn't.

Brian explained, "He was a lumberjack, which is why we call him 'Jack', even though that probably wasn't his real name. Back then people didn't have much regard for lumberjacks. They were considered less than human, because they spent so much time away from town, out in the woods, and lived pretty rough. So when they came into town, there was almost always a fight. Jack was knifed downstairs in the bar, and his body was dumped somewhere in the woods on the property. Or at least that's the story." It didn't seem as if Brian doubted the tale. "I was a skeptic before I started working here," he told me. "But not anymore. Jack's remains have never been found, so that's probably why he's still here," he added.

I asked Brian what kinds of things people have experienced in the restaurant.

"All kinds of stuff. Some of it can be explained—like sometimes a glass will fall off a shelf or lights will flicker, but things like that can happen anywhere, and the building is over a hundred years old. But there was one incident that nobody could ignore." Brian went on to tell me about how one night, when things were fairly slow, a customer witnessed four clear glass mugs, the heavy ones used for coffee drinks, fly off the shelf.

"The bartender wasn't in the room when it happened, but several customers swore to her that no one was standing anywhere near the shelf when they fell and shattered."

I've worked in restaurants and bars, and glasses don't generally come flying off the shelves—especially not four of them at once—so I was pretty impressed. We talked a little about some of the other places I visited while working on the book and a little bit about the hospitality business in general. Brian leaned in a little. "Then you'll probably appreciate this one. We had a waitress here that no one really liked—she just wasn't cut out to be a waitress, if you know what I mean."

Oh, most definitely. Waiting tables takes a very special personality and not everybody has it.

"Apparently, Jack didn't like her much either. It seemed as if every single time she passed by the broom it would fall on her. It's one of those old, wood-handled brooms. I mean, it wasn't heavy enough to hurt her, but there was no reason for it to fall on her *all the time.* Once, you could say, 'okay,' and shrug it off, but six or seven times? Eventually, she quit. That's about the only time Jack's been mean to anyone—and no one was upset to see her go."

By then, I was thoroughly intrigued and asked Brian if he'd ever had any experiences himself, since he used to live there.

"I never really saw anything, even though other people have claimed to see Jack, you know, like a misty apparition. There's one story of people seeing him on the dance floor downstairs, dancing with a woman dressed in Victorian-era clothes—so maybe he found some kind of happiness in the afterlife." Of course, being a romantic at heart, I couldn't help but smile a bit myself.

"But there were a couple of things that happened to me," Brian went on. "I was in the office upstairs—it was winter, and it can be a little drafty, but suddenly I was just freezing cold. The first thing that went through my head was *How in the heck did the window get open?* Only the window *wasn't* open. Some of the ghost hunters who have been out investigating the place say that the cold feeling you get is a ghost passing through you. I know that sounds a little silly." He shrugged. "All I know is that the window was closed and I was freezing."

"There was another time," Brian began with another story, "when I was locking up at night. The lights sometimes go on and off by themselves—and sometimes the radio stations change all by themselves. Or I guess it's Jack. Usually, the bartenders let him have his way and leave the station it changes too—if they don't, he just changes it back. Anyway," he said, resuming his original train of thought, "one night I was closing up, going through and turning off all the lights. The bar has track lighting, with each row of lights on its own switch. You flip one and all the lights on that track turn on or off. I was walking through and one single light turned on, lighting up the corner. I gotta tell you, that one freaked me out just a little."

There were other stories too. Jack has been known to move chairs and, once in a while, when the staff is clearing tables, they'll find a single shot of whiskey on a table that everyone is absolutely certain hadn't been occupied—at least not by any mortal patrons. Whiskey was Jack's drink, so sometimes when a regular customer comes in, they'll order a shot and leave it on the bar for Jack.

It's not just the patrons who appreciate Jack's presence. Brian told me that one day while he was still living on site, he and his aunt and uncle went out for a few hours to run errands. When they got back, they discovered a huge scorch mark on their apartment balcony. It looked like a bunch of leaves had caught fire—but just as mysteriously as it had started, it had stopped. There hadn't been any rain that day. "Somebody was looking out for us," Brian told me. "Maybe it was Jack."

Balcony of the apartment above the restaurant, where the Wagners found a mysterious scorch mark

He told me that when they were doing the groundbreaking for the Silo, his aunt and uncle half expected to find Jack's remains. They were relieved when they didn't. I could pretty easily see where that might not be the kind of thing one would want to find on their property, even if they already knew it was there.

Before I left, I asked Brian if it would be all right if I took a few photographs of the interior as well as the outside. He welcomed me to take as many pictures as I wanted and wished me a good rest of the day. The Grill House was definitely one of the friendliest places I'd visited—and I really do hope to go back to actually have a meal there.

SPOTLIGHT ON THE ADA WITCH

No book about haunted places in Michigan would be complete without at least some mention of the Ada Witch, who is perhaps one of western Michigan's more famous ghosts. It is unclear how the title "witch" got attached to her name—or even what her true name might be—but that's what locals call the adulterous specter who is believed to haunt Findlay Cemetery and Honeycreek Road, in Ada Township. Ada is a small community, located a little over ten miles east of Grand Rapids, and was first settled in 1821. It was in those early years that many believe the so-called "witch" met her tragic end, an end she accidentally set in motion.

One website dedicated exclusively to the legend of the Ada Witch claimed that she died in the year 1868. It is impossible to verify that date, however, as neither the woman's name nor the actual whereabouts of her grave are known for certain. We can only speculate.

The story says that the woman known as the Ada Witch was having an extramarital affair and would meet secretly with her lover in the marshes outside of town, near what is now Honeycreek Road. When her husband became suspicious of her late-night comings and goings, he followed her and caught her in the arms of her lover. In a jealous rage, the husband murdered first his wife and then the other man. During the struggle with his wife's lover, the husband was also fatally wounded and died a short while later. Perhaps that's why some people report seeing a mysterious ghostly woman wandering the area, and also a pair of ghostly men—maybe the men are the Ada Witch's husband and her lover.

The woman is believed to be buried in Findlay Cemetery, but nothing is noted in the stories about where either of the two men might

SPOTLIGHT ON THE ADA WITCH (CONTINUED)

have been interred. Although no one can prove that the gravestone is hers, locals believe that a broken old headstone near the back of Findlay Cemetery must be that of the legendary Ada Witch. Visitors often light candles or leave trinkets for her.

Several paranormal investigators have been to the cemetery and believe that it is indeed haunted. There is evidence in the form of orb photos and other unusual phenomena that have been caught on film and by digital cameras. Of course, just as there are many people who believe the story is true, there are just as many who think the Ada Witch is little more than an urban legend.

CHAPTER 14

GRAND HAVEN

KIRBY HOUSE

I left the Grill House in Allegan and headed north up M-40 through Holland and eventually up to Grand Haven. It was a perfect spring morning, ideal for an hour-long drive up the coast. Located on the shore of Lake Michigan, Grand Haven is a popular tourist destination, especially in summer when vacationers seek out the warm sandy beaches and romantic sunsets over Lake Michigan. In September, visitors can indulge in the delights of local wineries while they are in the midst of harvest season. For those who don't mind the cold, Grand Haven offers a Winterfest complete with dogsled races and other snow sports. February has its own winter fun when the city's streets are filled with ice sculptures during the Ice Festival.

But I was in western Michigan on the hunt for ghosts—or at least ghost stories—and Grand Haven seemed to have a lot to offer.

Navigating downtown Grand Haven proved a bit tricky, but in finally, I pulled up to the curb on Washington Street to park my car. I decided to head down to the Kirby first. Standing on the corner of Washington and Harbor Drive, the attractive two-story, gray-and-yellow building looked more like a modern pub than a place I would likely find ghosts. Still feeling hopeful, I went to the hostess stand and waited for someone to come over.

While I waited, I glanced through the menus. The Kirby House is actually three restaurants tucked into a single two-story building on the corner of Washington and Harbor Drive. There's the Kirby Grill, a casual family restaurant; 1872, a fine-dining restaurant; and K2, a wood-fired-oven pizzeria. I figured that even if there weren't any ghost stories to be found, lunch was definitely in order before I left Grand Haven!

But first to work. When the hostess, a young woman named Lillian, came my way, I gave her a friendly smile and explained why I was visiting.

"You should really talk to Tim," she advised me. "He'll be in later tonight if you want to come back."

I winced. I really had to get back on the road as soon as I wrapped up in Grand Haven, and while I had every intention of having lunch before I left, sticking around town until evening was out of the question.

"Have *you* ever seen anything?" I asked Lillian, hopefully. "Or maybe some of your customers or coworkers have told you about things they've seen or heard that might seem a little unusual?"

Lillian hesitated another second before deciding that it would probably be okay for her to take me downstairs to see where Emily's room used to be. Emily is the Kirby's resident spirit. She may have been a guest of the original Kirby Hotel—but that's just a guess; no one actually knows for sure who she was, just that she died in the building.

"Emily was coming down those steps, there." Lillian pointed to the wide staircase behind the hostess stand. "And she tripped on the hem of her gown and tumbled to her death."

Built in 1873 by renowned hotelman Edward Killean, the Kirby House was a hotel for many years before changing hands—and names. The building has had many owners and names over the last century before finally being purchased by Gregory Gilmore in 1989. Gilmore returned the establishment to its original name if not its original purpose, and it has been enjoying financial and culinary success ever since, despite—or perhaps because of—the ghost stories.

A few people claim to have seen Emily's ghost on the stairs, but more frequently, patrons and employees report hearing a small child's footsteps walking up and down the stairs or running around in the pizzeria upstairs. A few people have even reported seeing a little boy running around up there—others have said they simply saw a "shadow move," but when they turned around, no one was there.

Despite all the reports of ghostly experiences on the second floor, it was the basement Lillian wanted to show me. She got someone to cover her station for a few minutes and led the way, chatting as we went. "Customers over at the bar say all the time that they feel someone tugging at their legs or arms. Sometimes we tell her, 'Emily, stop it!'" Lillian told me, with as much conviction as if she were talking about a coworker—or maybe an errant child.

"Does that work?" I asked.

"Usually."

The storage area Lillian took me to is off-limits to the general public, but the basement itself is open to patrons. Following Lillian down the darkened wooden steps, I was hard-pressed not to feel a little bit of apprehension—but maybe that was just because I knew we were headed to Emily's room.

"A lot of people hear loud banging down here," Lillian said, as we stepped inside and she hit the light. The storage area looked pretty much like any restaurant's storeroom I'd ever been in before. "But whenever anyone goes to check it out, there's no one down here. There aren't any animals or anything either."

The place certainly looked clean enough; I wouldn't have suspected vermin. Besides, doesn't it take something bigger than a few mice to make "loud banging" noises?

"Some people won't come down here alone," Lillian told me. "I always feel like she's watching me, especially down in here." She led the way to the very back of the storeroom. By then we both had goose bumps. Lillian shivered. "Sometimes she turns the lights off and on, and doors sometimes open and shut by themselves. We've had a few things fall off shelves in the kitchen, but it's hard to tell if that's really Emily or just normal stuff that happens in a restaurant."

Later, while I was researching the Kirby House's history to write this chapter, I discovered an interesting connection between the restaurant and another one of Grand Haven's famous ghosts, the "Blue Man of Lake Forest Cemetery." Apparently, before Edward Killean built the Kirby House hotel, the land was owned by the Ferry family. Reverend William Ferry was one of Grand Haven's founding fathers. He built the very first permanent dwelling in town and lived there with his wife, Amanda, where the Kirby now stands. The Ferry's home burned to the ground in 1866, and the couple moved. A few years later, Reverend Ferry passed away and was buried on Founders' Hill, in the Lake Forest Cemetery. Local legend has it that his spirit appears to cemetery visitors as a glowing blue apparition. The story may just be an urban myth, but the Lake Forest Cemetery is on my list of places to visit the next time I'm in the area, as it is within easy driving distance of Grand Haven.

CHAPTER 15

PORTAGE

STUART MANOR

I wrapped up taking photographs of the Kirby Grill fairly quickly and was about to call my husband to let him know I would be home early when I noticed a voicemail message for me on my phone. It was from Alison Alexander, the cultural events coordinator for the city of Portage. Alison and I were supposed to have gotten together the day before at Celery Flats. She was calling back to see if I wanted to reschedule for that evening. So much for getting home early—then again, it isn't every day I get offered a private tour of a 150-year-old haunted house! So instead of telling my husband I'd be home early, I asked him to do the things on my list of household chores for the night and said I'd see him sometime after dinner. Portage is about 20 minutes south and slightly east of Kalamazoo, which makes it about 2½ hours west of metro Detroit.

Although Stuart Manor bears the name of former United States Senator Charles E. Stuart, it was actually built by William Welch in 1846, making it the oldest building I had toured so far. It also happens to be the oldest building still standing in Portage. The stately, white Greek Revival house was originally located on Stuart Avenue in downtown Portage, but in 1994 the city moved it to its current location in the Celery Flats Bicentennial Park. It has been fully renovated and outfitted with antique furnishings—except for the modern kitchen. The parks and recreation staff, who oversaw the restoration, needed a modern kitchen in the manor because of the plans to use the building for special events, such as Victorian-style afternoon teas, served on the weekends. In addition to city-sponsored events, Stuart Manor and several other historic buildings in Celery Flats are available for private rental. If I'd known that, I probably would have booked my bridal shower there. Not only would it have been Victorian-themed, but how much fun would it have been to tell people later about our party in a haunted house?

Celery Flats is described on Portage's website as "a park within a park." On one side of the road, visitors will find the Celery Flats Interpretive Center and Museum, which highlights the importance of celery farming to Kalamazoo County's history. On the other side of the road, park-goers can stroll along a paved walking path that curves past Stuart Manor, an old one-room schoolhouse (built in 1856), and a grain elevator, dating from 1931. In addition, many community and cultural events are scheduled at the Hayloft Theatre, a turn-of-the-century barn that was renovated into a theater in the late 1940s. Like Stuart Manor, it was also relocated to Celery Flats some years ago.

For visitors who just want to get a little closer to nature, there are numerous walking paths through the woods on the other side of the road (which is also a part of the park) and play areas for small children. Quite a few of Portage's residents were enjoying evening strolls along Portage Creek as I pulled into the Celery Flats parking lot for my meeting with Alison. With my camera in hand, I walked across the street where she met me at the door of Stuart Manor.

"I'm glad you were able to make it." She greeted me with a warm smile and welcomed me into the foyer. "We just had the house painted, so things still aren't quite all back to where they belong," she added apologetically.

"The house is beautiful," I told her. That wasn't just me being polite either. Stuart Manor might not be the biggest house I've ever been in—in fact, by modern standards, it's little more than average—but I could easily see it as the sort of place a senator had once called home.

Alison smiled and told me that she had been the person in charge of selecting the new paint scheme. "The walls were stark white before this. It was really boring. Not *all* of the new colors are strictly Victorian, but most of them are."

I was impressed and asked about what kind of research she had to do to come up with an authentic Victorian color scheme.

Alison laughed. "The paint store had a selection of historical colors; that made it a lot easier."

Of course, I wasn't actually there to talk about the décor, as lovely as it was. I was interested in the manor's history and its ghosts.

Alison showed me the portrait of Charles Stuart, which sits in the foyer. "We're not 100 percent positive it's him who haunts the place, but we refer to him as Charles anyway. Of course, we have a lot of antiques in here from other locations—nothing is original to the Stuart house. Sometimes when we bring new stuff in, we get a rash of paranormal activity." That, of course, was exactly what I'd heard from other people as well.

Portrait of Senator Charles E. Stuart in the foyer of Stuart Manor

"Charles doesn't like his picture being taken down," Alison told me. "It was one of the first things we put back after they painted. Weird stuff always seems to happen whenever we take it down. His portrait used to hang in the main room," she added. "But when we started having teas, we moved him to the foyer." We both agreed that it was a more dignified place for the former owner of Stuart Manor.

Alison showed me into the main room, which probably used to be a front parlor but was currently set up for afternoon tea. Several dining tables were set up around the large room, which also had a lovely upright piano along one wall.

"Do you want to sit down and talk first or see the rest of the house?"

"Would you mind showing me around?"

Before leaving the front room, Alison showed me the modernized kitchen and a little side room set up with one large dining table—which had a lot of china piled on top of it, waiting to be put back. "Sorry about the mess," she said again. The room used to be the family dining room but is now used mostly to store china and silver for afternoon tea.

As we headed toward the stairway, Alison warned me to watch my step. "They built steps pretty steep and narrow back then."

She wasn't kidding. I'm pretty short so I have small feet, and I still nearly tripped going up the narrow steps.

Alison filled me in on a little bit of trivia. "The house is built so that from the outside it only looks like a one-story house—that's why all the windows in the bedrooms sit so low on the wall."

The windows in the bedrooms were practically at knee level.

"Back then, you paid higher taxes for a two-story house," said Alison.

She led me into one of the bedrooms.

"We call this room the 'rope room.'" She showed me why. The mattress is held up by a net of ropes. "This is what they used before box springs," she told me. "This is the room that probably gets the most activity. We had groups of Civil War reenactors who rented out the grounds. One of the guys was changing up here, and he came bolting down the stairs. He said he would change anywhere but up here. He never told us why—just that he wasn't comfortable here. Another guy, on a different occasion, said that while he was up here changing clothes someone—or something—touched him. He was up here alone at the time. The story's gotten pretty exaggerated over time, and now people say he was pushed, but that wasn't the story he told at the time."

And that was what made the next part of Alison's recounting of events even more interesting.

"We've had a lot of paranormal investigators come through here," she said. "One of them had heard the story of the guy getting pushed, so when they came into this room, they asked the spirits 'Why did you push the soldier?' And the voice on the EVP (electronic voice phenomena) sounded so clear. 'I didn't,' it said."

Okay, I was definitely starting to think there might be something to the ghost at Stuart Manor.

"Sometimes the guys who are doing Civil War reenactments stay overnight. A few of them have sworn they heard someone walking around in the house, even though everyone else was asleep. We've had a bunch of reports from park rangers who come by at night on patrol and find lights turned on when there's no one staying here. They come in, turn the lights off, lock up—and when they swing back by later, the lights are on again. We finally just told them to go ahead and leave the lights on. It's easier on everybody."

Alison showed me the rest of the upstairs, and then we went back down to the main room to have a seat.

"That's Charles's chair," she told me, indicating a particular chair at the largest of the dining tables.

I decided not to sit there, just in case there really was something to the ghost story, and chose a seat on the other side of the table instead. Alison sat down next to me.

"How do you know it's his?" I wondered, remembering that none of the furniture was original to the house.

"We always find that chair pulled out," she explained. And then she smiled and said, "A lot of the people who have done work on the house have heard odd noises, but one time we had an electrician in, working on the light fixture in the original dining room." She nodded to the little room that houses the china cabinets. "He said he came out to get something from his toolbox and found Charles's chair pulled out. He didn't think much of it except that it was in his way, so he pushed it back into place and went back to work. He had his back turned to this room, so he didn't see what happened, but when he came back out to get something else, *all* the chairs were pulled out. Now he won't work over here unless I come over and keep him company."

I wasn't sure I blamed the guy. The rooms are directly adjacent to one another; if someone had been trying to put one over on the electrician, they would have to have been awfully quiet for him not to hear them. "Is anyone else uncomfortable being here by themselves?" I asked.

"I never have been," said Alison. "I figure it's just part of working in an old building. Sometimes we find the piano bench pulled out too," she said, indicating the piano I'd been admiring before. "I mean, it's possible that one of the guys working over here likes to play on his breaks or something, but . . ." She shrugged, leaving me to draw my own conclusions.

And while we were on the subject of chairs, Alison told me that during a private party held at the manor, one of the dining chairs had fallen over. No one was near it at the time; it just fell right on its side for no reason at all—or at least no earthly reason.

"Some of the paranormal investigators have said they found evidence that the schoolhouse is haunted, but I've never experienced anything there." She shrugged. Then she finished off our chat with the story of a mysterious figure people have seen near Stuart Manor, near city hall. "Over by the train tracks people see a woman coming out of the woods and getting into a coach—but then she vanishes. It only happens in the autumn."

I thanked Alison for her time, especially since she'd agreed to meet with me so late in the day and had given me such a great tour of the manor. As I was heading out, I drove past the railroad tracks where so many people say they've seen the ghostly woman boarding her coach. I didn't see anything, but Portage isn't that far from home, so I think I'll try again someday. Maybe next time I'll get lucky.

SPOTLIGHT ON NUNICA CEMETERY

When I was visiting with two friends of mine they told me a story about the Nunica Cemetery. A friend of theirs (someone they described as respectable, honest, and professional, the sort of person not prone to making things up) had relayed something unusual. He said that he and a friend were visiting the Nunica Cemetery. For some reason, one of the men had his father's cell phone in his pocket rather than his own. Perhaps his was broken, or maybe he'd just picked up his dad's by mistake.

As the two men were walking through the cemetery, they heard what they described as "old-time Gospel music"—the source was the dad's cell phone. But the thing was, Dad was an old-fashioned kind of man with a no-frills phone. He didn't even know how to download music to his phone, so there was no reason for it to be there—and no reason for the phone to have started playing anything anyway.

Neither of the ladies had any explanation for the strange occurrence but suggested I might want to check out the Nunica Cemetery. What I found was pretty interesting, because apparently, the Nunica Cemetery *does* have a reputation as being haunted—in fact, some people claim that it's western Michigan's most haunted cemetery. It's certainly one of the oldest I've ever visited.

There have been numerous reports of people hearing voices and feeling cold spots all over the cemetery grounds, as well as stories of a "lady in white," a ghostly apparition who is said to appear to visitors from time to time. Orbs and other ghostly phenomena have been photographed in the cemetery. While concrete documentation of the "lady in white" was scarce, I found a number of stories by people who claim to have felt or seen ghostly children running around the cemetery

grounds. Upon further investigation, I discovered that in the middle section of the cemetery, there were a lot of graves belonging to young children who likely died during an influenza outbreak in the 1920s.

Located in rural western Michigan, ten miles east of Grand Haven, the community of Nunica was founded in 1872. The Nunica Cemetery was established 11 years later, in 1883, and is one of two area graveyards. Like most cemeteries, there are posted "hours of operation," and the police will prosecute trespassers, because having a reputation as a haunted hotspot brings a lot of unwanted attention to the cemetery. Local officials don't object to respectful, responsible adults visiting during the daytime; it's just nighttime visits that are unwelcome. However, as at least one ghost hunter pointed out, if a place is haunted at night, it's just as haunted during the day. There's no reason not to stop in during the posted "open" times because if nothing else, the Nunica Cemetery is a beautiful old graveyard.

History buffs may want to look for Civil War veteran Henry E. Plant's gravestone while they're there. Plant, a soldier in the Union Army, received the Congressional Medal of Honor for rescuing his unit's colors from Confederate soldiers during a skirmish in 1865.

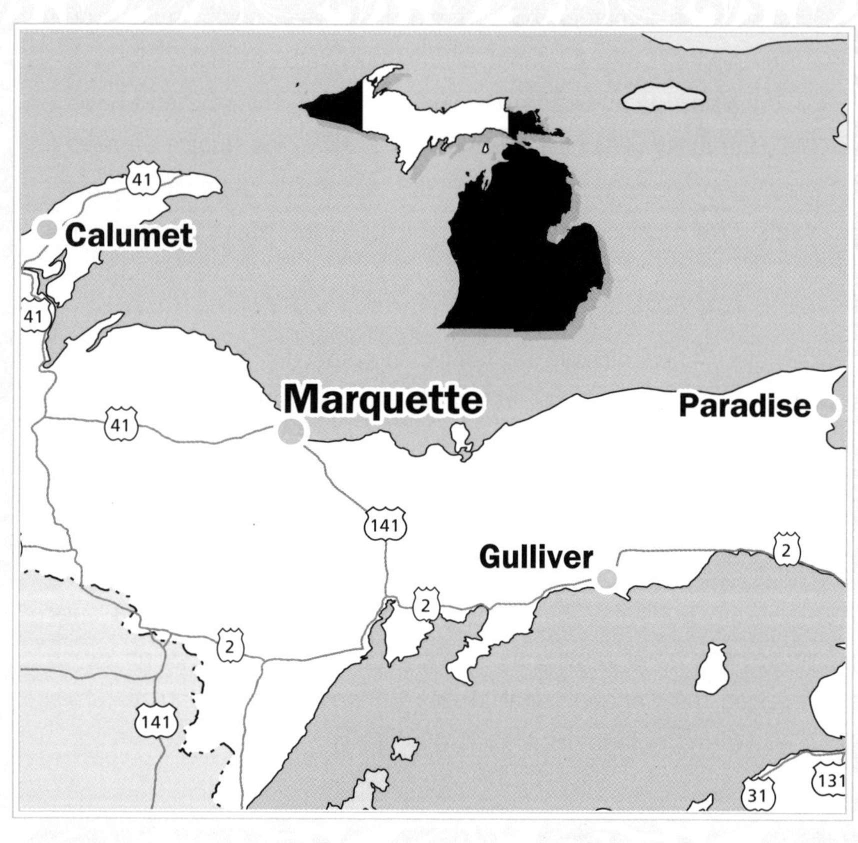
41
Calumet
41
Marquette
Paradise
41
141
Gulliver
2
2
2
141
31
131

UPPER PENINSULA

CHAPTER 16

GULLIVER

SEUL CHOIX POINTE LIGHTHOUSE

Although I've lived all my life in a state where more than 100 lighthouses dot the coastline, I had never actually visited one before venturing to Seul Choix Pointe, my first stop in the Upper Peninsula. I wasn't sure what to expect when I got there. The Point's 100-year-old lighthouse is reportedly one of the scariest haunted places in Michigan and was even featured on an episode of Fox Family's *Scariest Places on Earth*. Even coming straight from spending a relatively quiet night alone at the haunted Blue Pelican Inn (see Chapter 21), I was feeling some trepidation as I approached my next destination. The battered blue sign telling me that Seul Choix's historic lighthouse lay only 2 miles ahead did little to allay the feeling—neither did the slow drive up an old dirt road.

Seul Choix Pointe is a narrow, rocky stretch of land that juts out from Lake Michigan's northern shore into Seul Choix Bay, about a 2-hour drive east of St. Ignace. The bay received its name, which means "only choice," in the 1800s when a group of French fur traders took shelter there during a violent storm that threatened to capsize their small vessel. The bay was their "only choice" for safe refuge along the dangerous stretch of coast, which is known for its rocky shoreline and high waves.

Those same waves make Seul Choix Bay a popular destination for surfers. I found a group of young men out enjoying the waves and warm early autumn weather the day I visited the Point, and took a few minutes to talk to them. They didn't know anything about any ghosts at the lighthouse; they were just out to get in a few more days of lake surfing before the weather turned cold.

The Michigan State Congress commissioned the Seul Choix Pointe Lighthouse in 1886, but it took six years for it to become operational—I think sometimes we forget how much work went into building construction a century ago. The entire complex, which consists of the 79-foot light tower, family quarters, a steam fog signal and boiler house, stable, and several other buildings, wasn't completed until 1895. Additional living quarters were added in 1925. Back then, the Seul Choix Lighthouse was the only guiding light for ships along a hundred-mile stretch of treacherous coastline. The nearest towns are Gulliver—whose Historical Society, in cooperation with the Department of Natural Resources (DNR), oversees the upkeep of the lighthouse—and Manistique, a popular destination for boaters, campers, and hikers.

I arrived at the end of the long dirt road to find a well-kept yard, a brown brick house, and a classic white tower. Maybe it was the sunny weather, but I didn't feel as if I'd just pulled up in front of one of the "scariest places on earth." Wondering what I was really going to find, I headed over to the gift shop. Rather than asking about ghosts, my first question was, "How do you pronounce the name of this place?"

The young lady behind the counter laughed. It's a question she gets a lot. "The easiest way I know to pronounce it is Sis-shaw," she told me. After getting that cleared up, I explained that I was writing a book about haunted places in Michigan and wondered if she'd ever seen or heard anything unusual in the lighthouse. "Not personally," she said. Although several guests and other staff members told her they'd heard music, "like an old phonograph recording," playing in the lighthouse. She said that some people also report that electronic devices, like the digital camera I was carrying, stop working. "The batteries just die for no reason," she said.

I definitely hoped that wouldn't become a problem. Of course, I always carry extra batteries, just in case.

"If you really want some good stories, it's my mom you should talk to," she went on. "You can find her over at the lightkeeper's quarters."

I thanked her for her time and headed on over. The first thing that struck me when I walked into the house was how small the front parlor was. Yet at times in the lighthouse's history, not only did the lightkeeper and his family live there, but his assistant and his family resided in the small dwelling as well. That's four adults and as many as six children. The lightkeeper's home has been fully restored and is decorated with beautiful antique furniture—and seemed about as far from scary as I could imagine a place to be.

I quickly found Linda, the volunteer I was seeking, sitting in what had probably been a formal dining room. She looked up from her book and greeted me with a warm smile. As soon as I explained the reason for my visit, Linda invited me to have a seat with her so she could tell me about Captain Joseph Willie Townsend, the lighthouse's primary ghostly resident. She described him as a bit of a prankster, but not a ghost she or any of the other staff had ever been afraid of.

"He was originally from Bristol, England," she said. "Captain Townsend lived here from 1901 until he died of consumption in one of the upstairs bedrooms in 1910." Consumption is an old-fashioned term for tuberculosis. "Because he died in winter when the ground was too frozen to dig a grave, the Captain couldn't be buried straight away, and his body had to be stored in the basement for several months." Some of the paranormal investigators who have visited Seul Choix believe that might be why the captain's spirit remains "trapped" at the lighthouse.

Linda had her own ideas. She told me that the hauntings didn't really start until a couple of original pieces of furniture were brought up from storage when the lighthouse was last restored in the 1990s. One of the pieces in question is the kitchen table.

Kitchen at the Seul Choix Pointe Lighthouse, where staff frequently find silverware mysteriously moved around

"In England," Linda went on, "you set a table correctly by putting the knife and spoon on the left and the forks on the right." That's the opposite of the way we set a table here in the United States. "The Captain doesn't seem to like it when we set the table American style. We always find the silverware reversed, even though no one's been in the kitchen!" She laughed.

Like the other rooms, the kitchen is roped off so that visitors can look but not touch.

Numerous guests and most of the staff have smelled cigar smoke throughout the living quarters, even though no smoking is allowed in the building, and often there isn't anyone else around. Linda told me that, despite his health problems, Captain Townsend was a heavy cigar smoker, and it seems that even in death, he enjoys a good cigar.

In the mornings several volunteers have found a "crescent-shaped imprint" on the bedspread in the room they're pretty sure was the Captain's. "It looks like someone sat down right on the bed," Linda said. Some volunteers and visitors have reported seeing a man watching them from one of the windows, about halfway up the light tower—but no one was in the tower at the time.

Probably the eeriest of Linda's stories was one a guest told her. A woman was visiting the lighthouse sometime last year, and when she pulled in, she noticed a man wearing a heavy blue coat, walking across the yard to the lighthouse. Being friendly, she waved; he ignored her, but she didn't think that much of it. Like me, she went to the gift shop first, then went over to the lighthouse, looked around, and headed on her way. When she got home, the woman started doing some research on the lighthouse's history and realized that the man she'd seen in the yard was Captain Townsend! She contacted the lighthouse staff to tell them of her unusual encounter.

"Several people have seen a man wandering the grounds before," Linda told me, "but this was the first time someone positively identified the Captain, even though they didn't know who it was at the time."

I have to admit, hearing that gave me goosebumps!

In addition to Captain Townsend roaming the grounds, rearranging silverware, and ignoring no-smoking signs, volunteers have also found toys strewn all over the floor of the "children's bedroom" upstairs. Nothing had been out of place the night before, and, by all accounts, the lightkeeper's quarters had been locked up all night. Linda told me that she thinks the children's room might be haunted by the spirits of two of the little girls who grew up in the lighthouse. Although they grew up and moved away, both had recently passed on—and it was just about the time they died that the children's room became "active."

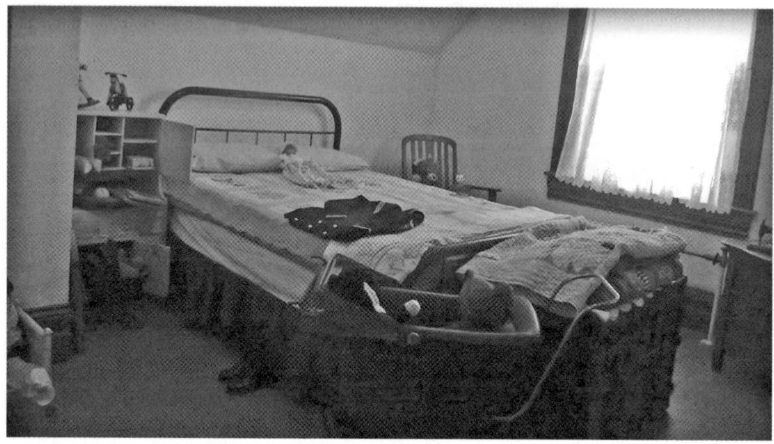

Childrens' bedroom at Seul Choix Pointe Lighthouse.

I thanked Linda for her time and went to have a look around for myself. Even though I had been told that a number of guests reported feeling the Captain's presence on the staircase, I didn't feel anything unusual. My camera continued to work too. I didn't smell cigar smoke or hear music. Even so, I appreciate antique furniture, so I enjoyed walking around the small house. And I appreciated the staff's sense of humor when I found the plastic Halloween skeleton hanging in an upstairs bedroom closet! I admit that it got me. I jumped.

When I came back downstairs, Linda let me step into the living room, which is normally roped off, so I could get a better picture of the antique organ, where the portraits of past lightkeepers are on display. She also invited me to climb the tower.

The lighthouse at Seul Choix is a working light station and one of the few where visitors are allowed to climb the tower. Of course, no one lives in the lightkeeper's quarters today; the station is automated. A hundred years ago, however, the light was fueled by oil, which had to be carried by hand up to the light at the top of the 79-foot tower. Every 2 hours, the lightkeeper or his assistant hauled two heavy metal buckets up a very narrow spiral staircase.

Because I'd never been to a lighthouse before, I decided to go ahead and make the climb—despite my horrible fear of heights. As I climbed the narrow metal stairs, I marveled at how a man twice my size had made the same trip four or five times a night, carrying heavy buckets filled with oil. I stopped at the midway point to catch my breath and enjoy the view from one of the windows—and got the distinct feeling that I was being watched. But no one else was in the tower with me. Of course, it might have been my imagination; I'd spent the last 40 minutes listening to ghost stories. Although my nerves threatened to get the better of me (because of the height, not the ghosts), I made it to the top. The view of the lake was spectacular. That alone made it all worthwhile.

The tower and lightkeeper's quarters are open to visitors from Memorial Day through mid-October. Guests are asked to make a small donation that goes to the Gulliver Historical Society to keep the lighthouse running. In addition to the lighthouse and gift shop, Seul Choix Pointe has a beautiful public beach, where I stopped to enjoy my lunch and take some more pictures before getting back on the road toward Marquette and the Landmark Inn.

INN

CHAPTER 17

MARQUETTE

LANDMARK INN

Although I had planned most of the places I would visit in advance, I had only made hotel reservations in a couple of hotels along the way—namely, the ones that were reputed to be haunted. The rest of the time, I sought out some roadside motels for simple accommodations and friendly, northern hospitality. Motel vacancies were easy to find, which allowed me a flexible schedule to enjoy the Upper Peninsula at my leisure. I tend to avoid the usual tourist attractions, but I did enjoy taking the time to hike through state-owned forests and long stretches of Lake Superior's magnificent coastline. I met a number of wonderful people along the way. One of them was a reference librarian in Marquette, who helped considerably with the research for this chapter. After all, librarians know everything (or so I've been told), and it is a fellow librarian who is said to haunt Marquette's historic Landmark Inn.

Originally called the Hotel Northland, the inn opened its doors in 1930. During its heyday, the Northland was host to A-list Hollywood talent, including Jimmy Stewart, Lee Remick, George C. Scott, Bud Abbot, and Lou Costello; and some musicians, including Duke Ellington and Louis Armstrong. Aviation legend Amelia Earhart is also on the list of former guests of the prestigious Hotel Northland. The room in which she stayed is now called the Earhart Room. Likewise, the room occupied by Abbot and Costello bears the famous comedians' names.

Unfortunately, the hotel fell into disrcpair during the 1970s and ultimately shut its doors in 1982. It remained closed until 1995 when Team Landmark, a company specializing in historic restoration, took on the monumental task of bringing the hotel back to its former splendor—and then some. The new owners had the idea to create a 62-room hotel that would feel like a bed-and-breakfast. Each room is uniquely decorated with antiques or replicas. Many of the rooms are themed, such as the Dandelion Cottage Room, with its white wicker furniture, or the North Woods Room, which is done up to look like a rustic log cabin—but still with all the amenities of a luxury hotel. Of special interest is the reputedly haunted Lilac Room on the hotel's sixth floor. The lilac room is called that because of the lilac-print wallpaper and lavender bedspread. (Unfortunately, I wasn't able to photograph the room when I visited because there was a guest staying there at the time—but I was able to sneak a peek inside when housekeeping went in to clean.)

I arrived in Marquette at about ten in the morning and headed straight to the Landmark Inn for brunch—and hopefully a few ghost stories. I have to admit, when I pulled up in front of the old, red-brick building, I didn't think I'd just arrived anywhere special. The exterior is anything *but* impressive. "Never judge a book by its cover," I reminded myself as I parked. And as soon as I stepped into the beautifully appointed lobby, I understood why the Landmark Inn is called the "jewel of downtown Marquette." The front lobby is everything you'd expect from an upscale hotel: white marble floors, dark wood-paneled walls, crystal chandeliers, and Oriental rugs.

I made my way to the main dining room but rather than being seated right away, I asked the hostess if she had a minute to talk. "I'm writing a book about haunted locations in Michigan," I explained, "and the Landmark Inn came up in my research into the Upper Peninsula's ghost stories."

She told me she was new at the hotel and hadn't seen or heard anything herself. "But everyone warns me not to go up to the sixth floor alone, especially at night," she added with a laugh. "I don't know if should take them seriously or not. They might just be 'hazing' the new girl."

Good point.

The hostess sat me in the section of a waitress who had been there for a while, and whom I hoped could help with material for this chapter. My server was busy when I first sat down, so I put in my order and waited until she delivered my scrambled eggs with salmon and capers before asking about the sixth floor's ghosts. She was a little reticent at first—not everyone who asks about the hotel's haunted history takes it seriously—but as I told her about some of the other places I'd visited on my trip, she relaxed and promised to come back and talk as soon as she got another guest's food out.

"I've never seen anything myself—but I don't go up there either," she said when she returned to talk. "I had a customer one morning, a man, who complained about how loud the guest in the room next to his was. He said he'd called the front desk several times to complain, but they didn't do anything. I had a minute, so walked over to the front desk to find out what was going on—we want our guests to be happy, and if someone isn't, we try to fix it. They checked the computer and said I must have gotten my customer's room number wrong, there was no one staying on either side of him. When I asked my customer to repeat his room number—and asked which room all the noise was coming from—I knew what the problem was. The noise was coming from the Lilac Room. I didn't want to tell him the room next to his was haunted, so I just suggested he ask for another room.

"I had another customer," she went on, lowering her voice just a little. "Another man. She, [the Lilac Room's ghost] doesn't like men very much. The first time he came down for breakfast, he commented about the blinds in his room. He'd drawn them before bed but was woken up in the morning by bright sun, because somehow the blinds had gotten opened in the middle of the night. I asked him what room he was in and he told me: the Lilac Room. I told him that if he wanted to, he could probably switch rooms, but he said it was no big deal. When he came down for breakfast the second morning, he said the same thing had happened. He drew the blinds before bed, but by morning, they'd mysteriously opened, letting in sunlight. The third night, he told me he *tied* the cord in place, so there was no way it could come loose in the middle of the night. But it did. In the morning the blinds were up again. He didn't know anything about our ghost, and I didn't tell him. He was checking out that day anyway."

The famous "Lilac Room" of the Landmark Inn

There's a reason the Lilac Room's resident specter acts out more toward male guests than women who stay there: The ghost is said to be that of a lovelorn librarian who died of a broken heart in the 1930s. She was in her 30s and had never been married. Today, we might not think much of a 30-year-old woman who is single, especially if she has a career, but 70 years ago, women married and started families young. Few had careers outside the home. A woman in her 30s would find herself with few prospects for a husband, which meant not only loneliness but social and financial insecurity as well. One can only imagine how happy the librarian must have been when she caught the eye—and heart—of a visiting crewman. He worked on one of the many iron ore freighters that regularly docked in Marquette. The city was, and still is, a major port town, with a bustling iron ore industry.

The librarian and her sailor courted, often meeting at the Hotel Northland, and eventually planned to marry—after he returned from one last voyage across Lake Superior. But he never came back. His ship was caught in a storm and sank, taking all hands to the bottom of the lake. The librarian never recovered from her broken heart and soon passed away herself. Many believe she returned to the inn after her death to wait for her love on the sixth floor, where they used to meet. Some guests have reported seeing a "ghostly woman" standing in the hall, staring out the window at Lake Superior.

Front desk personnel report calls coming from the Lilac Room when there are no guests staying there. Guests have said they get calls in the middle of the night, but when they pick up the phone, no one is there. Many have reported having trouble getting their room keys to work—and again, the bulk of the problems are reported by male visitors to the hotel.

The front desk clerk I spoke to said that it wasn't unusual for guests to ask to change rooms, sometimes in the middle of the night. "A lot of guests tell us they feel like someone is watching them, even though no one's there. One man said he felt the bed sag, like his wife was getting into bed with him—but then he realized she was still in the bathroom getting ready for bed."

On the other hand, the bartender I spoke to told me that while he knows some staff members refuse to go up to the sixth floor alone at night, he thinks they're just psyching themselves out. "It's dark up there at night, so it's easy to get freaked out, especially if you know the story." He told me that the only thing he found "weird" about the Lilac Room was the lavender color pallet. "No wonder guys don't like to stay there," he added.

Before I left, I asked the front desk manager if it would be all right to go up to the sixth floor myself, as long as I promised to be unobtrusive. When I got up there, the housekeeping staff were making their rounds, and I talked to a few of the ladies about the Lilac Room. They all reported being familiar with the ghost, but not frightened by her—then again, all of the housekeepers I talked to were women.

SPOTLIGHT ON ORB PHOTOS

There is a lot of debate over the phenomena of "orb" photos. Some people say that the only things being captured in the images are flecks of dust, insects, or moisture in the air. Ghost hunters believe that the orbs are connected to spirit manifestation, although even among paranormal researchers, there is some debate on exactly what causes the orbs to appear in photographs. Occasionally, people even claim to see orbs with the naked eye, such as the encounter Margaret Perry told me she had while eating her dinner in the Fenton Hotel's dining room.

With the advent of digital cameras, capturing orb images has become easier than ever. Paranormal researchers—and weekend ghost hunters—no longer have to wait for film to be developed; images can be checked on location. I sat down with paranormal investigator Tracy Harrell and asked her to share some of her ghost-hunting techniques, especially how she gets great orb photos—and how she knows they're really something supernatural and not just a fleck of dust in the air.

"Do you recommend any particular kind of camera?" I asked.

"I use a digital camera. Any camera with a flash will do; it doesn't have to be expensive. You can even get good results with your cell phone, as long as it has a flash."

"Any special tips for capturing orbs on camera?"

"It just takes some patience," she advised. "Sometimes you have to visit the same place more than once to capture something. It's best to go when it's dark out," she added. "Of course, it helps to go to a cemetery known for paranormal activity."

"What about trespassing laws?"

SPOTLIGHT ON ORB PHOTOS (CONTINUED)

"Unless there are hours posted or there's a locked gate, most cemeteries don't actually close after dark," she told me. "Out in the country, most people don't care, and most older cemeteries only have rudimentary fences around them. If somebody does ask, we tell them we're out ghost hunting and that's pretty much the end of it. I look at it this way," she went on, "who would the police rather have out there: a bunch of kids or us? Besides, when we're out, we're a pretty good deterrent to kids out getting drunk or whatever. We have cameras and we won't hesitate to take their photos to hand over to the police."

Obviously, there are some well-known cemeteries that should be avoided at night, such as the Lakeville Cemetery which has unfortunately become very popular with teenage miscreants. The most famous cemeteries often are patrolled by local police.

"But you don't have to go to a 'famous cemetery' to get good photos," Tracy assured me. Her favorite haunts are old country graveyards.

"I've always wondered," I said, "why is it better to go out after dark and to use a flash? Is it that ghosts only come out at night?"

"No, not at all. Orbs tend to be milky or pearlescent. If I were to take a picture in this room, and there was an orb, it might not show up." We were sitting in a well-lit hotel lobby. "It's not that it wouldn't be there, we just wouldn't be able to see it. Dim the lights and we could probably catch an orb on camera."

Tracy had some additional advice to pass on. "Always carry backup batteries, even if your batteries are brand new. Always document your trip. I keep a journal where I record the location, date, time, weather, if there are a lot of mosquitoes out and other details. That way, if you start going through your photos and discover a few really great shots, you

can go back to your notes to rule out any obvious 'natural' reasons for the orbs. That's why I always take multiple shots in rapid succession of the same place. If I get an orb or some other anomaly, like a mist or a streak of light that only shows up in one of the pictures, chances are it was just dust or a bug. It's also a good idea to take out more than one camera."

"Do you have any favorite cemeteries?" I asked her.

"Two that I can think of. There's one on Herbst Road, in Brighton, and one in Highland where I almost always get good photos. You should come along with us sometime," she added.

Now that's one invitation I can't wait to accept!

CHAPTER 18

CALUMET

CALUMET THEATRE

The Keweenaw Peninsula juts out approximately 40 miles into Lake Superior, making it the northernmost stretch of land in the Great Lake State. Not exactly a day trip for those of us who live in the southern part of Michigan, but it was more than worth the couple of hours it took me to get there from Marquette. The site of one of the most extensive deposits of copper in the world, Keweenaw's economy was once based solely on the mining industry. Later, lumber production took over as a major industry, but now, at the turn of the 21st century, the peninsula's economy centers around the tourist trade and jobs created by the two colleges that call Keweenaw home: the Michigan Technological University—or simply Michigan Tech—and Findlandia University. I scheduled an entire day in Keweenaw so I would have plenty of time to see the sights. In addition to the town of Calumet, there are a number of "ghost towns," which are abandoned copper-mining towns that are open to the public (although caution is advised when visiting them).

But before I went sightseeing, I had work to do! I had heard about the Calumet Theatre from an acquaintance who said he had attended a classical music concert there and had a "strange experience." Or, more accurately, the pianist had the experience and later told audience members about it. During the performance, the pianist "got the strangest look on her face," my acquaintance told me. She wasn't just getting into the music, "She was staring at something offstage." She explained later that she'd seen a "ghostly mist." Although the gentleman I spoke to hadn't seen anything, other audience members claimed to have seen it too. I was skeptical but certainly intrigued.

According to local legend, the Calumet Theatre is haunted by the late actress Madame Helena Modjeska (October 12, 1840–April 8, 1909), who even today is considered to be one of Poland's greatest stage actresses. She came to the United States in 1876 with her husband, Charles Bozenta Chlapowski, and although the couple settled in Southern California, Madame Modjeska toured all over the country. She appeared not only on stages in cities like New York and Chicago but also in rural communities as well, although, by all accounts, the Calumet Theatre was a prestigious opera house in its day.

The town, originally called Red Jacket, was settled in 1864 by workers from the Calumet and Hecla Mining Company, one of the largest copper mining operations in the United States at the time. In its heyday, Red Jacket was at the very heart of the peninsula's copper-mining region and enjoyed tremendous financial and cultural prosperity. The Red Jacket Opera House opened its doors on March 20, 1900, and when the village changed its name to Calumet in 1929, the opera house became the Calumet Theatre.

Calumet's downtown historic district consists of more than 60 buildings that have all been restored to look like they did at the turn of the last century. Anyone who appreciates old architecture or regional history will enjoy a stroll through downtown Calumet. The main attraction is definitely the beautiful Calumet Theatre, where Madame Modjeska appeared in a production of William Shakespeare's *The Taming of the Shrew* almost a hundred years ago. She wasn't the only star whose name graced the theater's marquee at the turn of the last century. Other famous performers included Lillian Russell, John Philip Sousa, Sarah Bernhardt, Douglas Fairbanks Sr., Lon

Chaney Sr., James O'Neill, and Frank Morgan. The theater still hosts productions, but in addition to professional shows and concerts, it is also the home of the Calumet High School's theater, band, and choir events.

The theater welcomes visitors year-round, offering guided tours during the summer months and allowing for self-guided tours. During the rest of the year, guests are welcome to have a look around on their own during regular box office hours. Because my trip up north was taken during the autumn, I'd called ahead and made an appointment with the theater's executive director, Laura Miller, who agreed to make some time to talk to me. She was on the phone when I arrived, so I asked the women working in the box office if they had ever had any encounters with the theater's resident ghosts.

"Oh yes," one of them said. "Practically everyone who works here has." Employees and patrons alike report seeing shadows or misty apparitions like the one I'd heard about. People often hear voices in the theater, even when no one else is working or run into "cold spots," a common phenomenon in reportedly haunted buildings.

"Nothing scary," a woman in the ticket booth told me. "Madame Modjeska just likes to make her presence known." It seemed like I had definitely come to the right place for ghost stories!

In addition to the famous Polish actress, there are several other specters reported to haunt the Calumet Theatre—at least according to the Internet. According to several websites that I found, the theater is the site of two murders. The first victim was supposedly a young girl named Elanda Rowe, whom local legend tells us was murdered "somewhere on the theater grounds." The second incident involves an unnamed gentleman who was supposedly murdered in the theater in 1903. Both ghosts are said to "scream at night," but no one I talked to has ever heard any screaming, and I wasn't able to find any factual evidence to back up either story. It seems like these reports are nothing but urban legends.

What I was able to verify was that in 1913, the Calumet Theatre was used as a temporary morgue for the bodies of 73 people, most of them children, who had died during the "Italian Hall Tragedy" on Christmas Eve of that year. Some 500 striking copper mine workers and their families were attending a Christmas Eve party on the second floor of the Italian Hall, which was located down the street from the Calumet Theatre. In the middle of the festivities, someone yelled "Fire!" and in the ensuing panic, people rushed for the single staircase leading to the ground floor. Many tripped and fell on the steep steps and were either trampled to death or suffocated as other people rushed over top of them, fleeing to safety. To this day, no one knows who called out the dire, and patently false warning, but when rescue workers cleared the bodies, they were removed to the nearby Red Jacket Opera House, now the Calumet Theatre. In 1941, folk singer Woody Guthrie wrote a song called "1913 Massacre" about the tragedy. Many of the miners blamed the incident on the company bosses, alleging that not only were they responsible for the cry of "fire," but that they had the doors of the hall locked. Although there remains no solid evidence to back up the allegation, the Italian Hall Tragedy is the subject of many books and a recent documentary.

Paranormal investigators often say that when people die sudden or traumatic deaths, their spirits have a tendency to get "stuck" here on earth and may attach themselves to places like the Calumet Theatre, where the bodies were laid out for some time after the tragedy at the Italian Hall. A number of psychic and paranormal investigators have visited Calumet and have recorded evidence of ghostly activity in the area of the theater that was used as a temporary morgue and also in the small memorial park that was erected in honor of the victims on the site where the Italian Hall once stood.

As soon as she was off the phone, Laura apologized for the delay and invited me back to her office so we could talk. She was very interested in the book I was writing and had personally accompanied a number of the paranormal teams that had investigated the Calumet Theatre. "They always get EVP and EMF readings on the stage," she told me.

Another place where there seems to be a lot of spirit activity is the second balcony, which for safety reasons is closed to visitors unless they are accompanied by a staff member. Several people have told Laura that they've heard "voices speaking in theater jargon," and have seen movement in the second balcony even when no one should be there. "We keep the doors locked," she added.

Haunted second balcony of the Calumet Theatre

Laura went on to tell me what had happened to one of the lighting technicians one night after the theater had hosted a performance by the Calumet High School drama department. "There's always a lot of activity after the high school has a performance here," she added. On that particular night, the theater's tech and drama department heads were cleaning up after the performance, and both swore they saw someone dart across the second balcony. Assuming it was just one of the students up there "exploring" where they shouldn't be, they called for the teenager to come down. No one answered. When the men went up to investigate, they found the doors locked and no one in sight. It was enough to convince them both that the theater was indeed haunted.

Laura told me that a few years ago she was visited by a woman from California who claimed to be psychic. According to her, "there are a lot of disquieted spirits" in the second balcony.

Even so, Laura repeated what the lady in the box office had said about not feeling uneasy in the theater, even when she's there all alone at night doing paperwork. "I work part-time for a couple of businesses in the historic district," she explained. "It's easy to let your imagination get the better of you when you're alone in some 100-year-old building with all the lights turned off. This is the only place I've never felt uncomfortable."

That was good to know, especially as Laura went on to tell me about some of her personal experiences with Madame Modjeska. She asked me if I'd noticed the portrait of Madame Modjeska hanging in the front lobby. Yes, I had.

"When I first started here, everyone warned me that Madame Modjeska doesn't like her portrait moved," said Laura. "Whenever someone does, something always happens to them. Never anything big," she added, telling me how one person who moved Madame Modjeska's portrait tripped on the steps and twisted her ankle. It might just have been a coincidence, but the staff always blames little mishaps like that on Madame

Modjeska's ghost. Heedless of the warning, Laura moved the actress's portrait during the Christmas season one year to put up a wreath. Shortly thereafter, she was working late in the box office by herself. "I was trying to get a ticket to print and it just wouldn't come out. Finally, on the third try, it printed." But instead of printing as it should have, the words "ghost writer" were written on the ticket, along with a picture of a Snoopy dog. Now, the printer *is* equipped to print words, but nowhere in its programming is there an image of Snoopy.

Why Snoopy? Laura showed me her keychain: it's a bronze Snoopy, her favorite *Peanuts* character. She thinks it was Madame Modjeska making herself known. "Just saying 'hello.'" But since that was the worst thing that happened to Laura after moving the portrait, the rest of the staff have decided she's the only one allowed to touch the picture. Apparently, Madame Modjeska likes Laura.

After we talked for a while, Laura showed me around the theater. When we went backstage she showed me the place where most people have reported seeing Madame Modjeska during performances. In fact, during one such performance in 1958, the famous actress's spirit was first seen by a young woman performing on the stage. The story the young actress told, is that she forgot her lines and that Madame Modjeska appeared to her and prompted her, getting her back on cue. No one else saw Madame Modjeska—or any other ghostly apparition—during that night's performance, but ever since that time countless visitors, actors, and staff members have seen the Polish diva. Typically, she appears in a purple gown.

Laura gave me a quick tour of the rest of the theater and let me take some photographs, but had to apologize for not having time to show me the second balcony. There was a performance that night, and she had to get back to work. That was all right, as I already had a lot to write about. I thanked her again for her time and headed out with a lot to think about.

In addition to my visit to Calumet that day, I toured the Eagle Harbor Lighthouse, which is also said to be haunted. Unfortunately, when I arrived I couldn't find anyone who had ever had any unusual experiences or who even knew the lighthouse was supposed to be the site of ghostly activity. Lesson learned: call ahead before trekking out into the middle of nowhere! Still, I didn't consider it a wasted trip. The lighthouse is rich in maritime history, and my kind tour guide suggested I take the scenic route up Brockway Mountain Drive before heading back down to Marquette. It was a perfect day for a drive, so I took him up on the suggestion and found the view of the lake and surrounding countryside to be absolutely breathtaking. It was definitely worth the 40 or so minutes it took me out of my way.

CHAPTER 19

PARADISE

WHITEFISH POINT LIGHTHOUSE AND SHIPWRECK MUSEUM

I absolutely believe in serendipity, that is, the occurrence of events by chance. I'm certain it was exactly that kind of good luck that led me to Whitefish Point.

The Point's lighthouse wasn't on the list of places I intended to visit on my week-long trek, but it turned into the best stop I had up north. I wouldn't have ended up there if it weren't for several random choices and a little bit of following my gut. I had some time to kill at the end of the week, so when I reached M-123, driving back from Calumet, I decided to head north instead of south. I had seen a couple of signs for Tahquamenon Falls, so I thought, "What the heck?" and decided to check them out. I'd heard they are spectacular. But I wouldn't know; I never made it that far!

M-123 runs through the Sault Ste. Marie State Forest and along the shore of Lake Superior, where it follows the shoreline of Whitefish Bay and cuts through the town of Paradise. The sun was beginning to set when I pulled into town, so I decided to find a place to stay for the night and drive out to the falls in the morning. I had quite a few choices for overnight accommodations: hotels, motels, or cabins. I opted for the Paradise Inn for no other reason than it was the most traditional-looking hotel in sight—although being within walking distance from a restaurant helped tip the scales in its favor.

When I handed over my driver's license, the gal behind the desk grinned; she'd grown up less than five miles from where I live. "So what brings you all the way up here?" she asked, as she handed it back. I really didn't look like the average tourist; Paradise is popular with hunters, birdwatchers, hikers, and fishermen. I looked a bit more like a hippie in my long silk skirt and blouse.

"I'm writing a book about haunted locations around the state," I explained.

She smiled again. "Oh, so you're here for Whitefish Point." It wasn't a question.

"No," I admitted. "But I'd love to hear more about it."

"You have *got* to go up to the lighthouse. We get those paranormal people out here all the time. A couple of years ago, those guys from the science fiction channel came out. They stayed right here!"

So much for my plans of taking a whole day just to relax and sightsee!

Whitefish Point juts out a few miles into the eastern end of Lake Superior, but it is an important turning point for shipping traffic in and out of the lake. It also marks the eastern end of an infamous 80-mile stretch of shoreline known as "Shipwreck Coast." Whitefish Point itself is sometimes called a "Graveyard of Ships," as nearly half of the ships that have been claimed by Lake Superior's unforgiving waters were lost within the vicinity of the Point. Little wonder the light station, established in 1849, is the oldest working lighthouse on Lake Superior.

Although I was familiar with the tragic story of the *Edmund Fitzgerald,* a freighter that went down in Lake Superior on November 10, 1975, I hadn't realized that the ship was lost less than 20 miles off Whitefish Point. All 29 crewmembers were lost; the story was put to music by Gordon Lightfoot in 1976. The Great Lakes Shipwreck Historical Society recovered the *Fitzgerald's* bronze bell in 1995, and it remains on exhibit in the Shipwreck Museum at Whitefish Point.

I arrived at my destination early the next morning and noticed a group of people hauling their gear out of the former Coast Guard Crew Quarters, now a fully operational bed-and-breakfast. I thought little of them or the amount of gear they were hauling out of the building—I've been known to pack a lot too!—and made my way up to the museum.

I hung near the back of the line so I could talk to the cashier without holding anybody up, and I have to admit I was surprised to find a *line* of people at 10 a.m. on a Monday late in September. As soon as I told the cashier about the book I was writing, she offered to call over to the Crew Quarters and see if someone could come talk to me. "Beth, our housekeeper, is the resident expert on ghosts around here!"

That sounded good to me. In the meantime, I paid the admission and had a look around the museum. When Beth arrived, we chatted a bit. She was warm and welcoming and she took me over to meet that group of people I'd seen leaving the Crew Quarters when I first arrived. Turns out they weren't just tourists; they were members of the Motor City Ghost Hunters, paranormal investigators based out of metro Detroit. The group had just finished up a weekend-long investigation of Whitefish Point. Beth told them about my book and introduced me to team leader and founder, John, lead investigator and "sensitive," Chass, as well as Tom, Kellie, and several other team members. Despite having been up late the night before, they were more than happy to talk to me about their experiences at Whitefish Point. John gave me his card and graciously invited me to email him if I had any questions. Like I said, serendipity. Whitefish Point wasn't on my list of places to visit, and if I'd turned right instead of left, I never would have ended up there. I made some great contacts and had a fantastic tour of the site, compliments of Beth.

That weekend had been the Motor City Ghost Hunters' fourth visit to Whitefish Point. They told me it was one of their favorite places to visit because every time they come up, they find something new. "It's like spirits are attracted to the place," John said. Both he and Beth speculated that spirits might be attracted to the lighthouse's beacon. It would seem logical that sailors would hone in on the light. But it's not just the ghosts of mariners lost to Lake Superior's icy waves that visitors have spotted at Whitefish Point. Guests staying overnight at the Crew Quarters have reported seeing apparitions of men dressed in Coast Guard uniforms. Doors in the old building are said to open and shut by themselves, and numerous visitors have reported being touched in the middle of the night—especially ladies staying in the downstairs bedrooms.

After chatting with the Ghost Hunters for a while, Beth offered to show me around. I was delighted to have a tour guide. The first place we went was the Crew Quarters, which aren't normally open to the public since there could be guests staying over, but after talking to the Ghost Hunters, I really wanted to see the building. Beth told me as we walked that her ghosts are "real pranksters." She calls her favorite ghost "Stinky" because of the strong cigar or pipe smell people report smelling in certain rooms of the Crew Quarters. The first time she smelled it, Beth was certain a guest had been smoking in one of the bathrooms, but no one even *had* a cigar or a pipe. She suspects that "Stinky" was one of the Coast Guard crewmembers who lived there almost 50 years ago. Beth spoke affectionately of the ghost. I was surprised by how many people I met during my trip up north genuinely enjoyed the presence of the spirits that had been reported where they worked.

"Stinky steals keys," Beth cautioned me, as we entered the building (I immediately made sure I knew where mine were!). "There's one set that I *still* haven't found. I'd like them back, please!" she added, just a little louder, not talking to me at all. "Sometimes things get moved around in the kitchen. I, or one of the guests, will put something on the table or the counter, and the next time we see it, it's in a drawer on the other side of the room, even though no one touched it or saw it move."

Beth led the way to the downstairs bedrooms where several guests had reported being touched in the middle of the night. "The guy down here really seems to like the ladies," she said. "One woman told me she thought her husband had come to bed because she felt his side of the bed sag and then she felt a hand on her back. But when she rolled over, she saw that her husband was still in the bathroom brushing his teeth."

After touring the Crew Quarters, Beth walked with me over to the lighthouse keeper's quarters. Although the lighthouse has seen many different keepers throughout the years, one of the most memorable was Captain Robert Carlson, who lived at Whitefish Point from 1903 until 1931. During much of that time, his granddaughter Bertha Endress Rollo (1910–2007) also lived there. During the 1980s, Mrs. Rollo worked with the historical society at Whitefish Point to restore the lighthouse to its former elegance. She donated much of the furniture and artwork that had belonged to her grandfather for the exhibits in the lightkeeper's quarters. There are many pictures of Mrs. Rollo as a young girl throughout the old family quarters in the lighthouse. As Beth pointed out, she is always smiling, so if perhaps her spirit has returned to its childhood home, there is little to be afraid of.

However, Beth said there was one room in the lighthouse that made her very uncomfortable. They call it the children's room; it's one of the upstairs bedrooms and is decorated with a crib, children's toys, and an old baby doll lying in a wooden cradle near the center of the room. "A lot of people say they see a child staring down at them from that window," Beth pointed to the window in question. "It could be a little girl or a little boy, but I think it's a little girl." She said she believed that the girl died in the room, although she has yet to uncover any concrete proof to support her theory. Certainly a lot of families lived in the lighthouse over the years. "There's just something about this room that I don't like," she said, again.

When Beth asked me if I felt it too, I had to confess that the room did make me a little uneasy, but then again, when you listen to ghost stories, it's easy to let your imagination run away with you. Or maybe it was just the antique doll in the room that gave me the willies; I've never liked old dolls. Beth told me that one morning she came in to discover that the cradle the doll rested in had mysteriously broken overnight. No one could figure out what had happened to make the wood crack like it did.

Finally, Beth took me over to the Great Lakes Shipwreck Museum, open May to October. She wanted to show me the exhibit about the SS *Myron,* which sank in 1919 off the coast of Whitefish Point. The bodies of the 17 crewmen who perished in the wreck washed ashore some months later; they are some of the very few men who have died on Lake Superior whose bodies were ever recovered. The men are buried in the Mission Hills

Cemetery in Bay Mills Township, one of the many cemeteries I visited on my trek across the Upper Peninsula. Beth told me that she always feels drawn to the *Myron's* exhibit, as though the spirits of those who died onboard are still clinging to the artifacts from the sunken ship. For my part, I felt a sense of sadness around all of the relics that had been recovered from the ships that went down near Whitefish Point as they reminded me of the tragic deaths of so many young men.

Ghostly phenomena have also been reported by guests and observed by members of the Motor City Ghost Hunters along the beach near Whitefish Point, where there is a memorial for the crewmen of the *Edmund Fitzgerald.* Many people have reported seeing apparitions or feeling as if they're being watched. A few people have even reported being touched while they walked along the beach.

If you visit the area also check out Tahquamenon Falls as I intended! In addition to the falls, the famous Pictured Rocks are located just a little farther down the shore from Whitefish Point. The Whitefish Point Bird Observatory is also great in warmer weather. The observatory is a 44-acre nature preserve that is a regular stop-over for migratory birds. Some of the species spotted there include eagles, hawks, falcons, owls, as well as geese and ducks. And when I come back, I know just where I'm going to stay—the Crew Quarters at Whitefish Point. After my stay at the Blue Pelican (see Chapter 21), I think I'm up for another night in a haunted inn.

SPOTLIGHT ON OUIJA BOARDS

According to the website for the Museum of Talking Boards (aka Ouija boards) "modern spiritualism" began in Hydesville, New York, in 1848, when sisters Kate and Margaret Fox (ages 12 and 15, respectively) claimed to have contacted the spirit of a dead salesman. The method they used for communing with their spirit friend is known as "rapping"—that is, getting the spirit to rap or knock on a table during a séance. Messages could be spelled out this way by asking a spirit to knock once for "A" twice for "B," and so on. Although Margaret later claimed the whole thing was just a hoax and even went so far as to demonstrate their methods to the public, the idea of speaking to the dead had already spread like wildfire across not only the United States but also Great Britain and other European countries.

Since the dawn of human history, the idea of spirits has fascinated people, and many have sought ways to communicate with those who have passed over to "the other side." Even after the Fox sisters were debunked, other mediums (called such because they acted as intermediaries between the living and the dead) continued to refine their methods of communicating with the deceased. Automatic writing replaced rapping; a pencil was attached to a small basket, and the medium would place his or her fingertips on it and allow the spirit to take over and write out their message. Automatic writing is still practiced by psychics today.

Eventually, the heart-shaped planchette, or "little plank," which was used to point to letters already printed out on a board, replaced the basket and pencil. This, of course, was the original Ouija board. The first patent for a commercially produced "talking board" was filed on May 28, 1890; it lists Elijah J. Bond as the inventor.

I came into contact with my first Ouija board when I was a teenager. Some of my friends were amazed by the thing, others were terrified. I have to admit, I was skeptical. Maybe that's why I never got any meaningful messages out of it. Nothing bad happened either, although certainly books and the Internet abound with stories of people who have had terrible, supposedly supernatural, experiences after playing with an Ouija board.

I haven't met up with any professional ghost hunters who use Ouija boards to communicate with spirits, but they do use some of the other methods used by early Spiritualist mediums. It is not uncommon for ghost hunters to ask spirits to knock or make a noise to indicate their presence during an investigation. In addition, some ghost hunters use a flashlight that has been lightly "tampered with," so that the connection between the bulb and battery is tenuous. Usually, it's just a matter of unscrewing the head so that it sits loosely on the base. Spirits are then asked to turn the flashlight on and off to let investigators know they are present and willing to communicate. Obviously, there is some question as to the accuracy of this method, but it's something to keep in mind if you decide to book a room at a known haunted hotel.

23
Petoskey
31
131
Central
Lake
Traverse City
75
31
131
127
MICHIGAN
75
10
10

NORTHERN MICHIGAN

CHAPTER 20

TRAVERSE CITY

MISSION TABLE AT BOWERS HARBOR INN

Probably best known for its wineries and annual Cherry Festival, Michigan's Traverse Bay area is also the home of the Mission Table (formerly called the Bowers Harbor Inn). At the time of my initial visit, Mission Table was an open-to-the-public restaurant but has since changed to being an event space. Located 20 minutes north of Traverse City on the coast of the Mission Point Peninsula, the Mission Table was the first stop on my ghost-hunting journey. I'd never sought out and visited reportedly haunted hotels or restaurants before, so I was a little nervous, unsure how my questions about specters would be received by staff, other guests, or owners. I was pleasantly surprised by the warm welcome I got at the Mission Table.

The drive up from Detroit was a long but pleasant one, and despite technical issues with my GPS, I had no difficulty locating the summer-retreat-turned-fine-dining-restaurant using the directions from their website (missiontable.net) as my only guide. The big blue building sits on the peninsula's main road, and though it is sheltered among the pine trees, it's not hard to miss. As I drove around to the parking lot, which looks out over a vineyard, I tried to remember as much as I could of the story of Genevieve Stickney, the Mission Table's resident spectral inhabitant.

Genevieve and her husband J. W. Stickney, then an

up-and-coming Chicago businessman, purchased the property in the late 1800s. At the time, the property consisted of an old farmhouse with a small orchard of fruit trees and was one of only a handful of homesteads on the peninsula. While J. W. built his million-dollar-plus lumber-and-steel empire, Genevieve went to work building her own successful, home-based business, making jams, jellies, and brandy. Eventually, the couple tore down the old farmhouse and built the mansion that stands on the property today, which they used as a summer retreat.

Sadly, a story that should have been happily-ever-after ended in betrayal and heartbreak. As she aged, Genevieve became increasingly overweight, which resulted not only in a decline in her health but increasing depression and emotional insecurity. One of the employees at the restaurant told me that at one point, Genevieve removed all of the mirrors on the property, presumably because she didn't want to look at herself anymore. Genevieve is often described by historians of the Inn as "bitter" and "jealous." It was during this period of physical and emotional decline that the Stickneys installed an elevator between the first and second floors because Genevieve was no longer able to climb the stairs. J. W. also hired a young nurse to assist his ailing wife, but it turned out the nurse was doing more to help J. W. than Genevieve. When J. W. passed away, Genevieve discovered that J. W. and the nurse had been carrying on an illicit affair behind her back for years. J. W. left his entire fortune to the nurse; Genevieve was left with only the house. She fell into a deep depression and eventually hanged herself from the rafters of the elevator.

After Genevieve's death, the property changed hands several times, with little if any reports of ghostly phenomena until 1959, when Jim and Fern Bryant purchased and renovated the old house and began converting it into a restaurant. Since then, there have been many sightings of Genevieve and even a few of J. W.

In 2006 John Carlson and Greg Lobdell, natives of Mission Point Peninsula, purchased the property and changed the name to the Mission Table. Carlson and Lobdell have worked closely with the Grand Traverse Regional Land Conservancy and Michigan Historic Preservation Network to preserve and protect the historic estate. In addition, Carlson and Lobdell instated a menu that includes local produce and spotlights locally brewed beer and wine from local wineries.

Arriving a little before three in the afternoon, I found the Mission Table Restaurant wasn't open yet, but the Jolly Pumpkin, a cozy little pub located at the rear of the main building, was serving lunch. I only wished I didn't have several more hours of driving ahead of me after I left Traverse City; I would have loved to have tried one of the local beers with my lunch. After ordering, I rather sheepishly gave my preplanned speech to my server: "My name's Helen, and I'm here because I'm writing a book about haunted places in Michigan . . . " I'd barely gotten the word "haunted" out of my mouth when my waitress's eyes lit up a bit and she smiled.

"I don't actually believe in ghosts," she told me quietly, "but this place is *definitely* haunted!" She promised she'd be back to talk to me as soon as she cashed out her other table. Well, that had gone better than I'd feared!

When my waitress returned, she told me that she'd spent a lot of time at what was then the Bowers Harbor Inn when she was younger. "My family used to bring me in here all the time, but I never saw or heard anything until I started working here a few months ago." She was careful to explain that everything she'd experienced could be explained as something *other* than Genevieve playing tricks. Lights flickering, even a beer tap going on by itself, could probably be explained away as "just one of those things."

But we both agreed that while flickering lights could be caused by a loose wire, beer taps don't usually just open up and start pouring on their own (she'd lost several pints of beer before she got it shut off again; it wasn't just a trickle). I've worked in restaurants myself and have poured beer from taps; they're not hard to pull, but they don't just fall open without help. Still, a loose beer tap isn't proof positive of Genevieve Stickney's afterlife presence in her home.

While I finished my lunch, my server went to find another waitress, Terri, who had been there longer and could tell me a lot more about Genevieve. Terri was getting ready for dinner service in the Mission Table restaurant, and I was invited to walk around upstairs before going over to talk to her.

The Jolly Pumpkin and Mission Table are connected through a short series of halls and stairs. I eagerly climbed the stairs and walked down a narrow hallway into the main building, the home Genevieve had shared with her husband, J.W., 100 years ago. Looking around, it was apparent that the owners had gone to great lengths to preserve much of the turn-of-the-19th-century charm, and it was easy to imagine what it must have been like for the Stickneys, during the happier days of their marriage, spending summers in this big, beautiful house on the lakeshore.

Even knowing the whole story I didn't feel anything especially ominous as I walked around upstairs—until I ducked into the ladies' room to change the batteries in my camera, which was starting to act up (most likely that had more to do with me than any ghosts!). As soon as I opened the ladies' room door, I immediately felt . . . *something.* Not quite a chill, but some sort of presence. Of course, I shrugged it off at once. Ever the skeptic, I figured it was my own mind playing tricks on me; after all, there I was prowling around all alone in an old, reputedly haunted building. So, convinced I was spooking myself, I switched out my camera's batteries and went downstairs to find Terri. She was in the main dining room setting up for an early dinner reservation, but more than happy to take a few minutes to talk to me.

Terri had been at the Mission Table "from the start," since the new owners took over in 2006—and from the very beginning, she'd been aware of Genevieve's presence in the old building. It started at one of their first staff meetings; the entire staff was assembled in the dining room, not far from where we were standing. "I was sitting right over there," she pointed to the far corner. "We were going over the menu and we were getting to taste everything when suddenly I felt a chill." Terri told me she initially shrugged it off, but then the woman sitting next to her asked "Do you feel that?" She'd felt the same icy chill.

Of course, it's an old building—it could just have been a draft, right?

Terri didn't think so, and by the time we were done talking, I was inclined to think there might be something to Genevieve's story too.

Terri told me that on another occasion, she and another waitress were standing upstairs near an ornate gold mirror that hung in the hallway, surrounded by old photographs. (According to several histories online, this mirror was purchased by the Stickneys because it seems to make people looking into it appear slimmer.) Terri and her coworker were standing on opposite sides of the mirror, but no one was in front of it. She describes what they both saw reflected in the mirror as "an aura" or a misty apparition. It passed across the mirror and vanished. Neither woman would have believed what they'd seen if someone else hadn't seen it too.

The next story Terri told me was about the ladies' room upstairs—the one I felt the presence in. Apparently, it is one of Genevieve's favorite haunts. One night when Terri was changing clothes after work in the ladies' room, she heard a loud rattling at the door of the outer room. (The ladies' lounge upstairs has two rooms—the lounge area and the restroom itself.). She shrugged it off, but upon exiting, an irate customer accused her of holding the door shut, preventing her from entering. Terri was nowhere near the door when the customer was trying to open it—and the door doesn't have a lock. She said Genevieve held the door shut on several people.

Terri told me that on another occasion, when she was serving a large party, one of the guests asked about the restaurant's haunted history, adding quite firmly that she doesn't believe in ghosts. Terri smiled and offered to tell her a few of her personal stories if the guest wanted to hear them, as soon as she had a minute. As dinner progressed into dessert, Terri served this particular woman a dish of frozen yogurt. The dish was cold, the yogurt was cold . . . and a moment after Terri set it in front of her customer, the dish shattered (no one was hurt). Terri jokingly "tsked" her customer, saying that was what she got for saying she didn't believe in ghosts. Then a thought occurred to her.

"Are you a nurse?" Terri asked her customer.

Puzzled by the odd question, the guest confirmed that yes, she was. Why?

Terri told her Genevieve's story. Apparently, the only time Genevieve is known to get at all nasty is when it comes to nurses. Little wonder, given her husband's infidelity.

Terri did tell me that she's never felt uncomfortable working in the old haunted restaurant; she tells Genevieve "good night" every day when she leaves work. "Gennie's more of a prankster than anything else," Terri expressed firmly. "She likes to play with the lights and the sound system." On any number of occasions, management has turned everything off for the night and gone upstairs to do the end-of-the-day paperwork, only to come back down later to find the lights and music back on, even though no one else was in the building and the doors were securely locked. Terri also told me that when the owners were renovating the landscaping a while back, workers dug up all sorts of jam and jelly jars—Genevieve had gotten quite eccentric in her later years and had taken to burying things around the property, apparently fearing people were trying to steal from her. Terri brought up the fact that it must have gotten awfully lonely out there in Genevieve's day—the peninsula wasn't always the tourist attraction it is today.

As we were talking about Genevieve, both Terri and I experienced goosebumps and would have sworn there was someone watching us. Proof of ghosts? Probably not, but it was enough to make me wonder.

SPOTLIGHT ON GHOST-HUNTING EQUIPMENT FOR THE WEEKEND GHOST HUNTER

Professional ghost hunters use some pretty sophisticated—and expensive—equipment. Chances are that's more of an investment than the average person wants to make. The good news is that the weekend ghost hunter can get by—and still get good results—with just a few ghost-hunting tools.

A good-quality digital camera is an absolute must, and the greater the resolution (the more pixels) the better. I use the camera that I bought a couple of years ago for vacations. It has the bonus of being small enough to fit easily in my purse. I use rechargeable batteries—but always carry a backup set (except for that one time at the Baldwin Theatre, the one time I needed them!). It is commonly reported that batteries die and electronics stop working in haunted places.

A second indispensable piece of equipment, according to everyone I spoke to, is a digital recorder. Most digital recorders are small and inexpensive. All of the ones I looked at had a record time of several hours.

Digital recorders are used to pick up EVPs, or electronic voice phenomena. Paranormal investigators frequently seem to record sounds and even voices on electronic devices, even when no sounds or voices were heard by the team members themselves during the investigation. Many paranormal teams post these recordings on their websites, allowing visitors to decide for themselves whether the "voices" caught on tape are real or just white noise.

A digital camera and digital recorder were the only pieces of equipment I took with me on my adventures around the state, and I really only used my digital recorder a few times. I left it on all night

when I stayed at the Blue Pelican—but if anyone was there, they didn't feel like talking to me.

Probably the next most popular ghost-hunting device is an EMF detector, which is used to detect electromagnetic fields. The theory is that where there are ghosts, the electromagnetic fields "spike." Other things can cause electromagnetic fields to jump too, such as outlets and major appliances. So you need to have an idea of what's in the area before jumping to conclusions. Natural and man-made (not paranormal) electromagnetic fields can cause people to have that same "eerie feeling" so many people get when they believe there are spirits nearby. Bearing in mind that you get what you pay for, weekend ghost hunters can purchase a decent EMF meter for $30–50 from most larger hardware stores. More expensive models can cost over $100.

A couple of the paranormal investigators I spoke to recommend using a 35mm camera, preferably loaded with black-and-white film, as a secondary source for ghostly images. If you're going out with a friend, it might be interesting to compare images taken with a digital camera and the old-fashioned way with film.

If you're more serious—or as you become more serious—you can add additional equipment to your ghost-hunting arsenal. Full-spectrum digital video cameras are popular, as are night vision or infrared camcorders.

It has been suggested to also document your adventures with pen and paper—or maybe start a ghost-hunting journal or blog.

CHAPTER 21

CENTRAL LAKE

BLUE PELICAN INN

I left the Mission Table late in the afternoon and headed for Central Lake and the Blue Pelican Inn, where I had a room reserved for the night. Central Lake is a small town in northern Michigan surrounded largely by farmland. It is located in what is known as the "chain of lakes," a system of small lakes in the Traverse Bay area that has become a popular destination for skiers, campers, hunters, and fishermen from across the Great Lake State. When I arrived at the Blue Pelican, I found the dining room filled with people who had been out on the golf course all afternoon and were just coming in for a bite to eat.

Ron, the manager on duty, told me that it was a fairly typical Tuesday night. The Blue Pelican's dining room is busy almost year-round, but, as it happened, I was the only overnight guest at the Inn. As soon as I told Ron that I was writing a book about ghosts, he asked me if I'd like to stay in Room Number One, or the Cherry Room, which is one of the Blue Pelican's reputedly most haunted rooms. I was more than up for it!

It was only after my dinner that I discovered I was the only guest at the inn and I would be staying overnight alone. None of the staff remains on the premises after dinner service is over. Was I scared? Not really. It gave me a great opportunity to do a little ghost-hunting of my own. If I did happen to hear or see something, I would know with certainty that it wasn't the housekeeper or manager making nightly rounds.

The Blue Pelican has gone by a variety of names over the years. Built in 1924 by local stonemasons Art Carpenter, Joe Blakely, and Jack Garrison, it was designed as a small hotel with the original structure featuring 22 guest rooms and a dining room. Currently, there are only seven guest bedrooms, each decorated with lovely antiques, hand-stitched quilts, and antique furniture. Ron told me I was free to wander into any of the other rooms I wanted to and mentioned that several employees and customers had told him they'd seen faces peering out the upstairs bedrooms when no one was staying in the rooms in question. One worker swore that he saw a face peering out at him through a window of a room that was boarded up at the time, due to renovation. Many guests have reported seeing the ghosts of the two people who are known to have died at the Blue Pelican.

During the Inn's early years, it was managed by Mr. and Mrs. Emmons Gill. Ron told me that Mrs. Gill died on the property in one of the upstairs bedrooms in the 1950s. It was shortly after her death that employees and guests began seeing ghosts at the inn. A few years ago, a guest was able to supply the inn's current owners, Chris and Merrie Corbett, with a photograph of Mrs. Gill, which sits in the wine case in the front lobby. Looking at Mrs. Gill's smiling face, it was difficult to be frightened of her ghost—if indeed she does haunt the place.

But Mrs. Gill wasn't the first person to die at the Blue Pelican Inn. The first documented death occurred in the 1930s when the young daughter of the inn's manager tripped on the hem of her dress while climbing down from a small second-story balcony and fell to her death. She was sneaking off to elope with her fiancé. Many guests have seen her wandering the upstairs hallway wearing a white dress, perhaps the wedding dress she never got to wear in life. Others have reported only a white cloud of mist, but they say they are sure it was a woman—or at least her spirit.

In addition to Mrs. Gill and the young bride, there are reports of the ghost of a little girl who has been seen looking out of an attic dormer. Upon investigation of the property's history, the Corbetts discovered that the inn had been used as a temporary school when the original Central Lake School burned down many years ago. Ron thought the little girl might have been one of the students who died in the fire. Perhaps she wanted to be with her classmates and followed them in death to the new school, but when they left, she lingered behind.

Other guests have reported seeing a little girl in the basement of the inn.

Heading up the stairs to my room for the first time, I got a sense of . . . something about halfway up the steps. It was the sort of something that you can't put a finger on but makes you think maybe the ghost stories are real. I stopped for a moment and looked around, but no one was watching me—no one was upstairs at all. The upstairs hallway is long, straight, and relatively narrow, with guest rooms along both sides. At one end of the hall is the door that leads to the balcony where the young bride lost her life in the 1930s—that door is securely locked.

"Rose Room" at the Blue Pelican Inn (the room I stayed in when I visited)

I quickly found my room and noticed that the doors have glass knobs, like the kind in the house I grew up in. The locks all require metal keys to open, not the card keys found at most hotels. After settling in, I explored the rest of the guest rooms, taking both my camera and audio recorder along with me. I didn't catch any strange sounds or orbs, but I did get that odd feeling again in Room Number Two, which is the other room with a lot of reported spectral activity.

Or maybe the ghost stories had gotten to me.

The Inn has been visited by a number of paranormal investigators over the years, including the young filmmaker, Cruce Grammatico. On YouTube, I discovered "Now You Know: The Hauntings at Blue Pelican Inn" after I came home from my trip up north. Cruce's "Blue Pelican Investigation" is now available for viewing on the inn's website. After watching it, I contacted the young filmmaker, who agreed to talk to me about his team's overnight stay in Central Lake. He said that once the employees and other guests began to clear out, the inn took on an "eerie" feeling. "The team felt nervous as they began their investigation, starting in the upstairs bedrooms," he told me.

The first thing that struck me when I was watching the video for the first time was that Cruce and his team got an EMF meter spike at exactly the same spot on the staircase as where I got my first sense that maybe the place really was haunted. Proof of ghosts? Probably not, but interesting nonetheless. EMF meters measure electromagnetic fields and are used by paranormal investigators to detect and track both explainable energy sources (such as power lines and household appliances) as well as fluctuations that cannot be easily explained. According to the paranormal researchers I talked to, a "spike" between 2.0 and 7.0 is considered indicative of spirit presence.

After investigating the upstairs bedrooms, Cruce told me he took his team into the basement banquet rooms. "I would be lying if I said it felt normal," he told me. "We started to do an

EVP session and immediately started hearing footsteps above us, but we were completely alone in the building."

EVP stands for electronic voice phenomena—all you need is a digital or tape recorder and a lot of patience. I tried a little EVP experiment myself when I stayed overnight at the Blue Pelican, leaving my digital recorder on all night while I slept, but the only thing I caught was my own snoring.

Cruce reports a much more exciting EVP session in which they heard a young boy say, "I'm here." According to owner Chris Bartlett, "You don't see much, but you hear a lot."

My only notable experience at the Blue Pelican Inn occurred just as I was getting ready for bed. It was late and everyone had gone home for the night. I'd also had enough time to poke around and get a good feel for the natural sounds of an old building—the house I grew up in is about as old as the Blue Pelican. I was just about to tuck in for the night when I heard a loud *click*. I recognized it immediately as the sound of one of the door handles turning, and it sounded like it was coming from one of the rooms down on the other end of the hall.

Except all of the doors were already open.

And I was alone at the Inn.

I left early the next morning, heading out long before any staff members arrived for lunch service. I had breakfast down the street and walked around downtown Central Lake for a while, enjoying a warm early autumn morning. Everyone I talked to knew they lived and worked just down the street from a haunted inn, but no one seemed bothered by the ghost stories.

SPOTLIGHT ON ELECTROMAGNETIC FIELDS AND GHOSTS

An electromagnetic field (or EMF) is simply a field of energy produced by electrically charged objects. Human beings emit electromagnetic fields, as does the earth itself. So do electrical appliances, both large and small. EMF detectors measure the amount of electromagnetic energy in a given area—typically a very small area.

Paranormal investigators are interested in electromagnetic fields for a couple of reason, but mainly use EMF meters to seek out and make note of man-made sources of electromagnetic energy, such as power outlets, electrical wiring, computer monitors, televisions, and household appliances. Why? Because many people are sensitive to electromagnetic energy. For those people, coming into contact with an electromagnetic field causes feelings of paranoia, like they're not alone, even in an empty room. This is the cause of that "eerie feeling" so many people report in supposedly haunted locations. Even people who are not particularly sensitive to electromagnetic energy experience these same feelings if they come into contact with a field strong enough. So, the first thing ghost hunters have to do when they arrive at a location to conduct an investigation is rule out natural or logical reasons for seemingly ghostly phenomena, including electromagnetic fields.

Although some people believe that spirits can also affect electromagnetic fields and cause them to fluctuate radically, causing a spike in the EMF meter's readout, this isn't necessarily the case. The truth is that no one knows what ghosts are made up of and what effect they have on the environment—or if they even exist at all. What an EMF meter will do is help investigators become better acquainted with their environment.

The first thing to do after purchasing an EMF meter is to become familiar with how it works. Simply practice by seeking out electromagnetic fields around your home in places you would expect to find them, such as around electrical outlets, in the kitchen, laundry room, and so on. Then walk to an area where you wouldn't expect to find much electromagnetic energy, and note the difference in the reading. Always take this kind of base reading when entering a new environment. Also, remember that EMF meters are sensitive to movement, so it's important to walk around *slowly*. Sudden movements will skew a meter's reading and you'll end up with false readings. For this reason, regardless of what they show us on television, EMF meters are not at all useful for "chasing ghosts." At best, an unexplained spike in a reading can tell researchers that *something* is going on around them—what that something is will probably always be up for debate.

CHAPTER 22

PETOSKEY

THE NOGGIN ROOM PUB AND STAFFORD'S PERRY HOTEL

I decided to take my husband with me to Petoskey on Michigan's northwest shore—on my last ghost-hunting adventure. The village was settled in 1879 and is named after the state's stone, a type of fossilized coral that is found in abundance there. It took us about 5 hours to drive from our suburban home up to Petoskey, but we couldn't have asked for a nicer day or a better place to visit. Petoskey is a quiet little town that looks very much like it did back at the turn of the last century. It is a favorite destination for vacationers year-round, especially those looking to escape the city and get out into nature—or people like me, looking for a good ghost story or two.

When we arrived my husband dutifully parked the car along one of the side streets across from the hotel, and we made our way around to the side entrance, where a short staircase led us down into the Noggin Room. I began by approaching the bartender that was on duty.

"We're haunted all right," he told me. "But I'm not really the person to ask." He took us over to the front desk because he thought the person who worked there knew more about ghosts than he did.

The lady on duty told us the same thing as the bartender. The hotel was definitely haunted, especially room number 310, but she didn't know much about it, just that the night auditor claimed to see stuff all the time.

"We have a book in the lobby you could read," she offered, helpfully.

Right. I decided to go back to the Noggin Room and try talking to another staff member instead. We had already decided we were going to stay for lunch anyway, so we sat down in the cozy, pub-like dining room to look over the menu. When a young waitress named Lauren came over to get our drink order, I explained the real reason for our visit.

"I don't suppose you've ever heard or seen anything?" I asked, hopefully.

I was starting to get discouraged by that point, although I wasn't about to admit to my husband that we may have just driven 6 hours for nothing. I had sort of sprung the trip on him at the last minute because I didn't want to make the drive alone if I didn't have to.

Lauren told me the same thing as everyone else. Yes, they were haunted, but, no, she didn't really know the details.

"But if you want to wait around a little, the night bartender, Michael, knows everything about this place," she said.

I looked at my husband, who just shrugged. It was already almost two o'clock. So we, or rather, I, decided we'd have a nice leisurely lunch, complete with appetizers and dessert. When the calamari arrived, we both decided we'd made the right call. Ghosts or not, the food was worth sticking around for.

A little before three o'clock, Lauren brought Michael over and introduced us. She told him I was looking for ghost stories about the hotel.

"We definitely have a few of those," Michael assured me, as he sat down with us. "I won't bore you with stuff you've probably already read; most of those predate me anyway," he said.

I took out my notepad and started taking notes, as Michael explained that the story he was about to tell was really about a certain "artifact"—but that to tell it right, he was going to have to start several days before he and some of his coworkers found it.

"It was February of 2010," he began, "during our Winter Blues Festival. We had balloons tied to all the chairs. I finished my shift, left work, and was headed out of town for the night. I'm driving along, and I get this frantic phone call from my manager. He told me he'd just turned off the last light and was getting ready to lock up for the night when suddenly he heard this loud 'pop' and then the pitter-patter of little feet running across the dining room floor. Sure enough, when he looked around, he saw that one of the balloons had popped. He was totally freaked out. I just laughed. I told him the ghosts were just saying 'hi' and not to worry about it. He said, 'I don't want them to say hi, I don't even want to know about them!' He was a total skeptic."

Michael explained that there were several ghosts who were supposed to haunt the hotel. Upstairs on the third, floor a woman named Doris is believed to haunt the library, although room 310 also seems to see a lot of supposedly paranormal activity. Besides Doris, there is a ghostly custodian named Keith, and a little girl who plays in the restaurant and occasionally roams the halls. Perhaps she was responsible for popping the balloon that freaked Michael's manager out so badly.

Michael told us that one of his coworkers had actually had a much closer encounter with the little girl. She told him that she noticed a little girl sitting in a chair in the hall, kicking her heels.

"She thought the little girl must be a guest," Michael said, "and so she stopped to ask if she was all right, but the girl didn't answer. She started back down the hall but glanced over her shoulder just a couple of seconds later, and the chair was empty. There was no sign of the little girl anywhere."

Okay, that would be much more likely to freak me out than a popped balloon!

"The incident with the balloon happened on a Tuesday," Michael continued. "The next night I was back at work. It was Lauren's first night," he added, glancing up at our waitress.

It was a fairly slow weekday afternoon, and she'd stuck around to listen to Michael's ghost stories too.

"So it was me and her and a couple of other wait staff," Michael continued, adding that the same manager who had called him the previous night after the balloon mysteriously popped was with them as well. "The place was closed and were all sitting up at the bar cashing out, and I was talking to them about the hotel's ghosts. Lauren was a little freaked out."

She nodded again. "Everybody's heard stories about this place, but working here . . . ?" she shrugged. "I wasn't really sure what to expect when I first started."

"I told her that the best thing to do was to just walk out into the restaurant and introduce herself," Michael said.

"I felt a little silly about walking into the middle of the restaurant and saying 'hi' to thin air," Lauren told us.

"I said I'd be right behind her," said Michael. "So she walks into the middle of the room and I'm with her; so is the other waitress who had closed with us and our manager. Well, we get out to about here," he nodded to a spot not too far from where we were sitting, "and all of a sudden something comes flying out from that area there." Michael pointed to what looked like a storage area nearby. "Lauren and the other waitress screamed, I started looking around trying to figure out what it was, and our manager was already back by the kitchen! It only took me a couple of seconds to find what had come flying out. It was one of the nozzles from the pop dispenser. We have two, and we take them off at night to soak them in a pitcher of water."

I nodded; I'd worked in enough restaurants to know that routine. If the nozzles aren't soaked nightly, they tend to clog up because the pop syrup builds up.

"The thing was," Michael went on, "when I found the nozzle on the floor, it was dry. We walked over and checked the pitcher of water the girls had put the nozzles into earlier, and there was only one in it. We knew the nozzle that had come flying at us had to have been one of the ones they'd put in to soak. It should have been wet."

I was definitely intrigued. Stafford's Perry Hotel doesn't advertise their ghost stories the way most of the other properties I had been to over the last few months did; all I'd been able to glean from the Internet were a few tantalizing hints that there might be something interesting going on here. It seemed I was right.

"The next few days were pretty quiet," Michael told us. "But that Saturday there were about eight of us sitting around after work. There were a bunch of new staff members, and we were talking about some of the weird stuff that had been going on all week, and one of the other staff members mentioned the library. So we all decided to go up there and have a look around. We got up there and the manager noticed a lump in the rug. We lifted up the rug and there was this huge wet spot. In the middle of the wet spot was a dry ring. In the middle of *that* was this little red book that was somehow dry. It wasn't an old book; it was printed in 1984 and it looked like it was in pretty good condition."

Third-floor library at Stafford's Perry Hotel—where staff members found the mysterious red book

Michael got out his cell phone and showed us a picture of a small dark-red book. The title was clear: *You Can Live Forever in Paradise on Earth.* He said that the picture he had pulled up to show me wasn't actually taken on the night the book was found, because, at the time, no one thought it was that unusual.

"The only 'odd' thing was that the book wasn't marked with the hotel's stamp," said Michael, "but we just figured it must belong to a guest, that maybe somebody's kid was playing a prank or something, hiding one of his parents' books under the rug. I put the book on the shelf over the fireplace, with a set of big blue encyclopedias. Then I kind of jokingly said something like, 'Hey, Doris, if you wanted us to have this, just leave it here, and I'll come back and get it tomorrow.' We all laughed a little and then went home."

Michael told me that the next day, the book was gone. They didn't really think much of it. Whoever it belonged to must have gone into the library, found it, and taken it home.

The next few months passed uneventfully, but then in May, Michael said he was hanging out at a friend's house after work when one of the waitresses called him, "freaking out."

"She kept saying, 'It's back, it's back!'" he told us. "I asked her, 'What's back?' She sent me this picture." He flipped through his phone to pull up a photo of the little red book wedged into a water pitcher. "The story I got," Michael explained, "was that she and the manager mentioned before were sitting up by the bar talking after work. The woman who called me said she felt something behind her. She and the manager both looked and saw this dark mist—which isn't that unusual, a lot of people have seen it down here."

I had to say that someone who works in a haunted building would call seeing a dark mist floating across the room "nothing unusual."

Michael laughed and went on with his story. "After they saw the mist, they decided it was a good time to finish up and go home. They were just getting the last of their work done when they turned back to the bar and saw the book. That's when they called me, just totally freaking out."

Michael said that after they took the book out of the pitcher, they noticed first that the book was only damp, so it couldn't have been sitting in the water pitcher unnoticed for any length of time, or it would have been soaked. They also noticed that there was a hole through the "o" in "you."

"They laid the book on a paper towel and put it behind the blender, out of sight," Michael continued. "When they came back in the next day, the book was gone. Now, the only people who knew about it besides them were the two front desk guys, who said they didn't touch it, and me, and I wasn't here. This place is locked up at night, so it's not like a guest could have come down and somehow found it. We had no explanation for why or how it went missing."

He added that one of the front desk guys told him that he'd come down to the restaurant around 6 a.m., to get a cup of coffee before going home, and he didn't remember seeing the book.

Now, by this time, Michael explained, he was starting to wonder if maybe someone was pulling a prank. After all, the same manager who claimed not to want anything to do with the ghosts had been there both times this little red book was found. *He* noticed the lump in the rug, and *he* was there when they found the book in the pitcher. Was that too much of a coincidence, or were the ghosts trying to make a believer out of a skeptic?

That summer passed peacefully, but on October 15, one of the business partners called Michael into the office and asked him to have a seat.

"And he opens up his desk drawer, and there's the little red book," Michael told us. "He'd heard stories about the book circulating among the staff and wanted to know if the book he'd found was *the* little red book everyone was talking about. I looked at it. It was bent, from when someone—or maybe something—had shoved it into the water pitcher, and there was the hole. I asked him where in the world he'd found it."

The man told Michael he found the book in the dumpster, sitting right on top of some white trash bags. The hotel only uses clear or black bags. They decided that if it was a hoax, it was an extremely elaborate one, and if it wasn't . . . well. Maybe it was easier to blame it on an ordinary human prankster.

The book remains in the business partner's desk for safekeeping. Or does it?

Before he left us, Michael told us about the ghost of a former custodian, a man named Keith, who haunts the second floor. The story goes that Keith loved the hotel, even though he often got stuck with the kind of grunt jobs nobody else wanted. Once, he even got accidently locked out of the building while cleaning windows on the second floor. I was sure the story was going to end badly—but a guest noticed Keith up there and he was let back in, no harm done.

Sometime after that, Keith was said to have remarked to one of the managers about how he would always take care of the place, because he was so grateful to them for giving him a job when nobody else would. I didn't get Keith's back story, just that whatever it was, he had said that working at the hotel had really given him a new lease on life.

A week or so after remarking that he would "always" take care of the hotel, Keith passed away. After that, it seemed as if windows were frequently—and mysteriously—found open on the second floor. A guest even caught what appeared to be an image of a ghostly figure outside a second-floor guest room window. Michael had a copy of it on his phone and showed me. It was difficult to tell what the image was, but it was certainly unusual.

CHAPTER 23

PETOSKEY

CITY PARK GRILL

After we left the Noggin Room, we went up to the third floor of the hotel, and I took a couple of photos of the library, and then we walked around a little outside. The Perry Hotel overlooks the bay, and it was a beautiful day. My husband put a few more coins in the meter while I stood looking out over the water, admiring the view. One of the waitresses from the Noggin Room came out to have a cigarette and joined me.

"You're the lady writing about the ghosts, right?" she asked.

I smiled. "That's me."

"Well, you know where you really ought to go since you're in town, is the City Park Grill."

I almost laughed. That was where we were supposed to have ended up. "How do we get there?" "Just go down the street, through the park, and make a left." She pointed. The City Park Grill was hardly a quarter of a mile from where we were standing.

"You should also check out the Mitchel Street Pub," the waitress advised me. "I hear it's pretty haunted too."

Armed with two good leads and knowing I had only one chapter left to write, we set off. Since it was the closest place—and because I was fascinated with the bar's history—we set off toward the City Park Grill first.

The pub was originally constructed in 1875 by Alanso McCarty as a mens-only billiard hall, serving fine cigars, wine, and liquor to local clientele. In 1888, Frank J. Gruclich purchased the billiard hall, adding food to the menu and changing the name from McCarthy Hall to the Annex. At the time, it was adjacent to the Cushman Hotel. Gruclich had a patio built into the east side of the building, and inside he added a stately, 32-foot, solid mahogany bar. That bar remains to this day.

Nine years later, in 1897, Gruclich passed away, and Frank Fotchman became the new owner of the business. Frank expanded the business, buying up the land just east of the patio, putting in a bowling alley in the basement, and opening up the Grill Café, in July of 1910. Shortly thereafter, and into the 1920s, one of his regular summer customers was Ernest Hemingway. The Annex bar mentioned in Hemingway's short story "Gentleman of the World" is indeed the Annex bar in Petoskey.

But it isn't Hemingway's ghost who is said to haunt the City Park Grill; it is the spirit of Frank Fotchman whom employees and customers alike claim to see—or more often hear. The local story has it that Frank hanged himself in the basement in 1932. No one knows why, but most say that Frank poured his heart and soul into the business, and maybe that's why so many people believe that he is still there to this day.

We walked in and I asked the hostess if there happened to be anyone around who could give us a couple of minutes to talk about Frank's ghost. She didn't seem particularly fazed by the request and went to find her manager, who "can probably tell you more than me," she said.

A few minutes later, the assistant manager, Matt, came out to greet us. He was intrigued by the idea of *Ghost Hunting Michigan.*

"I just wish I had more I could tell you," he said, explaining that he had only worked at the City Park Grill for a couple of years.

"You have to have heard something in two years," I replied.

"There's the usual stuff, glasses falling off bar shelves and breaking, stuff seeming to move all on its own—things that might be nothing. There was this one time, though," he admitted. "I was working late with a couple of other people. We'd just closed up and locked the doors, and one of the guys I was working with thought he saw someone passed out, probably drunk, in the hallway." He nodded toward the long hall that we had seen when we first came in. "It happens once in a while," Matt explained. "Anyway, we went back to wake the guy up and see if he was able to walk home, or if maybe he was staying at the hotel, or did he need a cab or whatever—only there wasn't anybody there. The front door was locked," he repeated. "We looked all over the bar, but couldn't find any sign of any customers. That's the only time I've ever had anything like that happen."

According to Matt, for most of the employees at the City Park Grill, it's the basement that makes them the most uncomfortable. Of course, it's hard to say whether that's because Frank's ghost still lingers or because everyone in town knows that's where he killed himself. But Matt described the basement as "pretty eerie."

"One day I was up here working by myself, and I swear I heard footsteps coming up from the basement." He showed us the door that leads to the basement on the other side of the dining room. "I opened it up and looked down—no one was there. I shut the door again and tried to go back to work. I'm not the only person who hears weird sounds coming from the basement once in a while."

Matt called over one of the waitresses and asked her if she had ever seen or heard anything unusual.

"The chair," she told me.

"The chair?"

"I was working closing one night. I was out here cleaning up, and the cook was in the kitchen. I swept, wiped down all the tables, and pushed the chairs in, just like every night. Then I had to go into the back for something, I don't remember what now. But when I came back to the dining room, there was this one chair pulled out, like someone had been sitting in it. I didn't really think much of it at the time," she admitted. "I just pushed it back in and finished up what I had to do in the back. Later, I came up for something else—and the chair was pulled back out again. No one else had been out in the dining room, and the front door was locked. I stayed in the back until it was time to go home."

That would definitely have been enough to make me not want to be alone in the dining room either.

"There's one other story I remember someone telling me," Matt went on. "One of the bartenders told me he'd seen this little girl, poking her head out from around the corner. He thought it looked a little strange, so he went to check it out. He said there was no one there; it was like the kid had just vanished."

If we hadn't had to get back on the road, I would have stayed to have a drink at the same bar where literary giant Hemingway once sat. Instead, I thanked Matt and his staff for their time, took a couple of photographs, and we walked back to our car. We're definitely going to head back up to Petoskey sometime—or at least I will.

Frank's portrait and newspaper clippings on the wall of the City Park Grill

SPOTLIGHT ON MACKINAC ISLAND

I also visited Mackinac Island, which is supposed to be one of the most haunted places in Michigan. It seemed little wonder, given the age of the settlement. Even before Europeans arrived in 1634, the island was inhabited by members of the Ojibwa tribe, who considered the island to be the home of the "Gitche Manitou," or "Great Spirit." Unfortunately, while I had a great stay, the first two days I was there, the only people I was able to talk to were seasonal employees who either didn't know anything about the island's hauntings, or who didn't want to talk about it. On my last day, I decided to get up early, walk into town, and talk to a few of the locals. They were much more helpful.

The island is a popular summer destination for Michiganders, most of whom come to get away from the city for a few hours and indulge in Mackinac's most famous commodity: fudge. I could easily have gained ten pounds in one weekend alone if it weren't for all the walking I did, and my family would not have let me back in the door if I hadn't brought home a half-pound of each of everybody's favorite flavors. Mackinac is accessible only by boat or small plane, and there are no motor vehicles permitted on the island. To get around, visitors walk, rent bicycles, or take a horse-drawn cab. Horses can also be rented for exploring the island's many beaches and trails. While many people only go for a day trip, I visited in the off-season and got a great deal on my hotel room, proving that it doesn't have to be as costly as a friend had warned me it would be. I stayed at the Mission Point Resort, which is so well known for its ghosts that the resort was visited by the crew of the SyFy channel's *Ghost Hunters* in March 2011.

There are a lot of ghost stories circulating about the Mission Point Resort, which was originally built in 1825 by Christian missionaries

SPOTLIGHT ON MACKINAC ISLAND (CONTINUED)

William and Amanda Ferry. Many guests report seeing the spirits of children who died on the property during a tuberculosis outbreak in the mission's early days. The infected children were quarantined in a cellar to protect the rest of the population; few survived. The resort's most famous spirit, however, is probably Harvey, a lovelorn man who jumped to his death from one of the cliffs behind the resort after his girlfriend broke off their relationship. Harvey's room was located in what is now staff quarters, but guests have reported seeing him wandering other parts of the hotel as well. In fact, I mentioned this project to an acquaintance when I returned from my trip to Mackinac, and he said a friend of his worked a summer at Mission Point a few years ago and declared the place "totally freaky."

When I visited the Baldwin Theatre, administrative manager Vonnie Miller told me a story about her experiences on Mackinac Island. When Vonnie was a teenager, she visited the island and snuck out one night after curfew. She couldn't recall exactly where in town she'd been, just that she looked up to see a man standing under a light, watching her. She was sure she was going to get caught—only a second later, the man was gone. Vonnie told me that after she saw that, she hurried back to where she was staying.

I did a little nighttime investigating at Fort Mackinac when I was on the island. The British built the fort in 1780, and it was the scene of two battles during the War of 1812. Allegedly, the spirits of many long-dead soldiers still patrol the fields behind the fort at night, perhaps not realizing that they're dead and the war long over. I didn't see any ghosts, just a few bats . . . but it was kind of dark, and I'd just taken the walking ghost tour, so maybe I was more than just a little bit nervous being up there all by myself at 11 o'clock at night.

Mackinac Jane's Audio Tours offers two summer tours, one biking, and one walking which offer an excellent way to get to know the island. The Mission Point Resort has started a yearly tradition of hosting a "haunted weekend" in September. Guests booked into the special package are given the opportunity to participate in a real paranormal investigation and decide for themselves if the place is actually haunted.

When I go back for another visit, I'm not only going to schedule more time to explore the rest of the island, but I'll probably stay at the Cloghaun Inn, a little bed-and-breakfast in the heart of town. According to the owner of the coffee shop where I ate breakfast on my last day, the bed-and-breakfast is "definitely haunted." I stopped by to talk to the owners before I left, but they were in the middle of breakfast service, and I had to catch my ferry home. Not that I'm *looking* for an excuse to go back or anything. . . .

GHOST-HUNTING TRAVEL GUIDE

VISITING THE HAUNTED SITES

Below is the contact information for all the places I visited while researching this book.

SOUTHEASTERN MICHIGAN

The Whitney
4421 Woodward Avenue
Detroit, MI 48201
(313) 513-2273
thewhitney.com
Please see website for current hours.

Marlow's Chill and Grill
23307 Telegraph Road
Brownstown, MI 48314
(734) 362-0988

Camp Ticonderoga
5725 Rochester Road
Troy, MI 48058
(248) 509-7676
campticonderoga.com

Baldwin Theatre
415 South Lafayette Avenue
Royal Oak, MI 48067
(248) 541-6430 (Box office)
stagecrafters.org

Bone Heads BBQ
10256 Willis Road
Willis, MI 48191
(734) 461-9250
boneheadsinc.com

Holly Antiques (formerly Main Street Antiques)
118 South Saginaw Street
Holly, MI 48442
(248) 634-1800
hollyantiques.com

Fenton Hotel Tavern
302 North Leroy Street
Fenton, MI 48430
(810) 750-9563
fentonhotel.com

THUMB AREA

Forester Township Cemetery
2631 Lakeshore Road
Forester Township, MI
The cemetery is located on Lakeshore Road, just north of Forester Road.

WESTERN MICHIGAN

Henderson Castle
100 Monroe Street
Kalamazoo, MI, 49006
(269) 344-1827
hendersoncastle.com

The National House Inn
102 South Park View
Marshall, MI 19068
(269) 781-7374
nationalhouseinn.com

Regent Theatre
211 Trowbridge Street
Allegan, MI 49010
(269) 673-2737
alleganregent.com

Grill House Restaurant
1071 32nd Street
Allegan, MI 49010
(269) 686-9192
grillhouse.net

Kirby House Restaurant
2 Washington Street
Grand Haven, MI 49417
(616) 846-3299
thegilmorecollection.com/kirby.house

Stuart Manor
7340 Garden Lane
Portage, MI 49024
(269) 329-4522
portagemi.gov

UPPER PENINSULA

Seul Choix Pointe Lighthouse
Gulliver Historical Society
9055 Seul Choux Point Road
Gulliver, MI 49840
(906) 283-3183
greatlakelighthouse.com

Landmark Inn
230 North Front Street
Marquette, MI 49855
(906) 228-2580
thelandmarkinn.com

Calumet Theatre
340 Sixth Street
Calumet, MI 49913
(906) 337-2610
calumettheatre.com

Whitefish Point Lighthouse and Shipwreck Museum
18335 North Whitefish Point Road
Paradise, MI 49768
(888) 429-3747
shipwreckmuseum.com

NORTHERN MICHIGAN

Mission Table at Bowers Harbor Inn
13512 Peninsula Drive
Traverse City, MI 49686
(231) 944-6984
Website: missiontable.net
Please see website for current hours and other details.

Blue Pelican Inn
2535 North Main Street
Central Lake, MI 49622
(231) 544-2583
thebluepelican.com

Noggin Room and Stafford's Perry Hotel
100 Lewis Street
Petoskey, MI 49770
(231) 622-8887

City Park Grill
432 East Lake Street
Petoskey, MI 49770
(231) 347-0101
cityparkgrill.com

MORE HAUNTED PLACES TO VISIT

Cadieux Café, 4300 Cadieux Road, Detroit, MI 48224, (313) 882-8560

Scarab Club, 217 Farnsworth Street, Detroit, MI 48202, (313) 306-9191

Detroit Opera House, 1526 Broadway Street, Detroit, MI 48226, (313) 237-7464

Bonstelle Theatre, 3424 Woodward Avenue, Detroit, MI 48201, (313) 577-2960

Fort Wayne, 6325 West Jefferson Avenue, Detroit, MI 48209, (313) 628-0796

Birmingham Theater, 211 South Woodward Avenue, Birmingham, MI 48009, (248) 723-6230

Lakeville Yacht Club, 1318 Rochester Road, Leonard, MI 48367, (248) 572-6999

Capitol Theatre, 140 East 2nd Street, Flint, MI 48502, (810) 767-5141

Greenfield Village and Henry Ford Museum, 20900 Oakwood Boulevard, Dearborn, MI 48124, (313) 982-6001

NCG Cinemas-Midland, 6540 Cinema Drive, Midland, MI 48642, (989) 839-2663

Murray Hotel, 7260 Main Street, Mackinac Island, MI 49757, (906) 847-3360

Grand Hotel, 286 Grand Avenue, Mackinac Island, MI 49757, (800) 334-7263

Island House Hotel, 6966 Main Street, Mackinac Island, MI 49757, (906) 847-3347

Ste. Anne's Catholic Church, 6836 Main Street, Mackinac Island, MI 49757, (906) 847-3507

Cloghaun Bed-and-Breakfast, 7504 Market Street, Mackinac Island, MI 49757, (906) 847-3885

Crimson and Clover Floral and Gifts, 68085 South Main Street, Richmond, MI 48062, (586) 727-0963

White Horse Inn, 1 East High Street, Metamora, MI 48455, (810) 678-2276

Legendz Bar, 1631 Garfield Street, Port Huron, MI 48060, (810) 987-0856

Stafford's Weathervane Restaurant, 106 Pine River Lane, Charlevoix, MI 49720, (231) 547-4311

Big Bay Lighthouse Bed-and-Breakfast, 4674 County Road Kcb, Big Bay, MI 49808, (906) 345-9957

Old Presque Isle Lighthouse, 4500 East Grand Lake Road, Presque Isle, MI, on Lake Huron, (989) 595-2752

Fairchild Theatre Auditorium, 542 Auditorium Road (inside the Wharton Center), Michigan State University, East Lansing, MI, (517) 335-1855

Tawas Point Lighthouse, 686 Tawas Beach Road, East Tawas, MI 48730, (362) 590-1554

Grosvenor House Museum, 211 Maumee Steet, Jonesville, MI 49250-1246, (517) 849-9596

Bond Street Mansion, Niles, MI 49120 (the house and crypt are private land, but it is believed that the ghostly aspirations of the former owners cross the street between the home and graveyard on a nightly basis).

River Raisin National Battlefield, 333 North Dixie Highway, Monroe, MI 48162, (734) 243-7136

Nunica Bar, 17040 112th Avenue, Nunica, MI 49448, (616) 837-9752

Purple Rose Theatre, 137 Park Street, Chelsea, MI 48118, (734) 433-7673

Howell Opera House, 123 West Grand River Avenue, Howell, MI 48843, (517) 540-0065

Oak Hill Cemetery Battle Creek, home of the weeping statue known as "Crying Mary" (also the final resting place of Sojourner Truth) 255 South Avenue, Battle Creek, MI 49014, (269) 964-7321

Griswold Auditorium, 401 Hubbard Street, Allegan, MI 49010, (269) 673-3456

The Civic Theatre, 329 South Park Street, Kalamazoo, MI 49007, (269) 343-2280

Old Jail Museum, 113 Walnut Street, Allegan, MI 4901, (269) 673-8292

Allegan Elks Lodge, 701 Marshall Street, Allegan, MI 49010, (269) 673-5656

Air Zoo, 6151 Portage Road, Portage, MI 49002, (269) 382-6555

Forest Roberts Theatre, 1401 Presque Isle Avenue, Marquette Township, MI 49855, (906) 227-2553

Antlers Restaurant, 804 East Portage Avenue, Sault Ste. Marie, MI 49783, (906) 253-1728. Site of the 1913 Italian Hall Disaster in Calumet. There is a large historic marker in the park on the corner of Elm and 7th street, which is where the Italian Hall once stood.

Point Iroquois Lighthouse, open May 28 through October 13, 12942 West Lakeshore Drive, Brimley, MI 49715, (906) 437-5272

Cadillac House Inn & Tavern, 5502 Main Street, Lexington, MI 48450, (810) 359-7201

House of Ludington, 223 Ludington Street, Escanaba, MI 49829, (906) 786-6300

Big Rapids Cinema, 213 South Michigan Avenue, Big Rapids, MI 49307, (231) 844-6284

Beckwith Theatre, 100 New York Avenue, Dowagiac, MI 49047, (269) 782-7653

Ramsdell Theatre, 101 Maple Street, Manistee, MI 49660, (231) 398-9770

ABOUT the AUTHOR

Helen Pattskyn first became interested in the paranormal at an early age and has since read many books on ghosts, hauntings, and strange phenomena. Helen has enjoyed visiting cemeteries, old buildings, and other reportedly haunted locations, approaching each with an open mind. With an educational background in library science, Helen spends her time as a writer and artist, attending local science fiction conventions.

The Story of AdventureKEEN

We are an independent nature and outdoor activity publisher. Our founding dates back more than 40 years, guided then and now by our love of being in the woods and on the water, by our passion for reading and books, and by the sense of wonder and discovery made possible by spending time recreating outdoors in beautiful places.

It is our mission to share that wonder and fun with our readers, especially with those who haven't yet experienced all the physical and mental health benefits that nature and outdoor activity can bring.

In addition, we strive to teach about responsible recreation so that the natural resources and habitats we cherish and rely upon will be available for future generations.

We are a small team deeply rooted in the places where we live and work. We have been shaped by our communities of origin—primarily Birmingham, Alabama; Cincinnati, Ohio; and the northern suburbs of Minneapolis, Minnesota. Drawing on the decades of experience of our staff and our awareness of the industry, the marketplace, and the world at large, we have shaped a unique vision and mission for a company that serves our readers and authors.

We hope to meet you out on the trail someday.

#bewellbeoutdoors